You Have To Love It

The Value of Classical Music

Kevin Don Levellie

Third Edition

ISBN 978-1-304-10276-8

Contact Information:
Kevin Don Levellie
17475 E 390th Road, Paris Il 61944
217-463-8770 or 217-712-1287
KDLevellie@gmail.com
On Facebook as Kevin Levellie
Blog at http://levellies.blogspot.com;

More books on music available through www.lulu.com include:

What Does Bach Prove?

Southern Gospel Music What Makes It Southern

The Book of Opinions and Observations (contains chapters on music)

The Christmas Season (This book contains chapters on Christmas music)

To Jenessa,
Daniel
and Alyssa,
who appear on the
back cover with me,
and
who I hope
will come to
love this music.

INTRODUCTION

This is a book of enthusiasms. It is not about what Classical Music **is**, but about what it **does** for me. My interest is in experiencing music rather than in explaining it in terms of the kinds of chords used, the progression of ideas or the perfection of the development of the method employed. All that I have known is that I have heard this, and it has made a difference in my life.

By extension, then, my book is about what this music could do for you. It is a record of my personal journey to and through these enthusiasms, not as a patter, but as an example of what this can do. It won't teach much in an academic sense, nor will it examine, in psychological terms, all the mechanisms of music and the mind, but it will show a heart which has been enlarged and encouraged by a great art form. That's really the point of life, anyway, that we should do something with and from our hearts.

We are all more than our functions and beliefs. We are unique persons, created in the image of God. I would be such a person, even if I did not believe in the nature of man as a unique creation rather than as a chance happening. Functionally, I operate as a husband, father, grandfather, son, and preacher, among many other things. Apart from function, I have artistic and cultural interests. These are a large part of what I am, too. I am a Christian, and while my beliefs don't create truth, they do shape my identity and perceptions.

Everything we think and do and experience contributes to our totality. Because I am speaking of Classical Music, it does not mean that I am trying to promote some sort of elitism. Even though Classical Music seems elitist, it is an interest no more valid than an interest in popular forms of music such as Country or Rock. Choosing to participate in no music at all is also a valid choice. I make no case for relative precedence or importance. I'm only telling you what I love and leaving you free to find your own love.

Classical Music. I've loved it for years. It is always experienced by the heart, even more than with the ears. That's why you have to love it. It is my contention that instead of teaching people to know or identify the arts, it would be better to help them find what they love in them. **Then**, they'll know them, because people never forget what they love.

Love is a rather strong word, and normally it should be reserved for our relationship to other persons. If there was a contest, there is no way that music could possibly compete with my God, my wife, my children and grandchildren, my extended family and my church family, but I use the word, love, to show that I have a relationship with music. It is not merely a dead thing that I use to my own pleasure. It is something that I come to with my heart, and not merely my head.

Liking approves, but love engages and relates. Love means that we receive, we are responsive, we reciprocate. This is true no matter what kind of music a person loves. By our regard, we relate the music to our lives. Every thing we relate to enlarges rather than diminishes our lives.

It is love because it is a human connection. We are dealing with the continued life force of the music's creators which rings out every time it is heard as well as that of the performers who invest themselves in it. I have a higher regard for music than I have for other "things" in this world. Music is one of the few things we have on this earth which we will have in heaven. Individual pieces may not be eternal, but music is.

There have been many books written on music "appreciation". As of 17 January 2013, when I started this book, Amazon was handling 8564 titles under the heading of "Music Appreciation". And, of course, there all kinds of books of analysis of specific musical forms and composers as well as books about the psychology of music, but what about simply loving the music? Love trumps understanding every time. Love is the ultimate value.

The book started out as a collection of isolated scraps of paper. From time to time, I would write down an idea or include it in my Book Of Opinions. Then, all the scraps somehow got together and got organized. They were no longer thoughts in isolation, but parts of an entire schematic.

I acquired the term "schematic", as I'm using it in this book, from an article by John Sloboda, entitled "Brain Waves To The Heart", published in the November 1998 issue of the BBC Music Magazine. This one article explained my relationship to music better than anything else I have ever read. I'm not going to quote or plagiarize his article, but I am going to "borrow" two terms he used, schematic and veridical, and shape them for my own use to explain my love for and use of this music.

We normally think of a schematic as a drawing which shows everything in a manufactured item, specifying all the parts and drawing out all the connections in their correct relations and proportions. By following it out, a technician could manufacture that item or a repairman could repair it, because the entire plan of the item is laid bare in a systematic manner in which nothing is concealed or left to chance.

I have a schematic inside myself of the culture of my heart. It includes the music which is a part of me. It is a construct containing the entire body of my musical preferences placed on a sort of grid of genres, types and styles. It is not merely a catalogue listing works I like, but a pattern of the kinds of works I like. It shows what I will have an immediate relationship to when I heard it even for the first time. It puts everything in relationship to myself and what I like.

For example, the symphony is in general my favorite form of Classical Music. If a piece is a symphony, it is more likely to find inclusion in my system, even if I have never heard it before or if it is a style I am not in sync with. The schematic doesn't create my preferences, but it brings them out into the open so that I am aware of them.

Sometimes I happen to like a work which is outside the network of my likes or which is unlike anything else in my schematic. Since we are not machines or computers, we are not bound to our own preferences to the exclusion of all else. To borrow another term from the BBC article, these isolated pieces which are not a part of the genres in my schematic would be called "veridical". They are specific likes rather than generic ones. A person has both a pattern of preferences and solitary enthusiasms which have no company.

There is no way of predicting a veridical liking. It would be impossible to do so, since they don't fit any pre-existing pattern in our preferences and are a matter of serendipity beyond analysis or forecast, so we will put them to one side and examine the schematic for the most part. It's just good to be aware that they are there and that, in liking something out of our ordinary, we are not abandoning or betraying anything in ourselves or in our schematic.

This is my second attempt to analyze a music form through the medium of words. My goal is not to untangle the knot of what music is, but to gain understanding of myself and my own interior. We are boxes and are filled with boxes. This is partially the heritage of our Western experience, but also it is how it is with us from the way we were created. In terms of our immediate culture, Western thinking is categorical. I want to understand the unique categories of Classical Music and the functions of the music.

I'll be making observations and constructing points of analysis based only on what I have actually heard, not what I have read about. Real knowledge of music comes from listening. There is not a day which goes by in which I do not listen to several hours of music. It accompanies me when I read and study, and as I drive down the road. I don't think I could operate in a world of silence. I love music.

I suppose I'm a strange bird in my musical tastes. I love populist Christian music in the forms of Southern Gospel and Black Gospel. You can add Elvis as a complete genre of his own and some of the older country music such as that of Hank Williams, Sr. and Bob Wills to my schematic.

Then, there's Classical. I've found that liking one thing doesn't exclude me from liking something else, even if the two likes exist in isolation from one another without common intersections. They may exclude one another, but I don't have to exclude any of them.

I have been attending the Contemporary Music Festival at Indiana State University in Terre Haute every fall since 2009. I would have started doing it a decade earlier when we first moved into the area, had I known of it, but I didn't find out about it until then. A few times, I have spoken with the faculty member who is one of the organizers of the event. The first time we talked, she made the comment that she was somewhat amazed that a preacher would like Contemporary Music. It was unexpected to her, but I enjoyed it long before I started attending the festival. In a sense this book, although not undertaken to specifically answer her, is my telling what I get out of this. We ought to get something out of art.

Why shouldn't I like Classical Music? Other preachers champion baseball teams and play golf prodigiously, and those things have nothing to do with the actual functioning of the ministry. Sports isn't the only legitimate interest allowed to a preacher. Having a vocation still leaves us free to enjoy ourselves within the limits of the moral.

I would have to say that, with a few exceptions, I enjoy the entire spectrum of what is called Classical Music. The examination of my schematic is the heart of this book, and I have done my best to present it as clearly as possible.

By the way, when I speak of music, if it is unidentified further than that, it will be Classical Music which is being referred to.

Classical Music does something for me. It does something to me. That's why I've chosen to spend the time it has taken to crystallize and record my thoughts through the writing of this book.

This book, rather than being an examination of Classical Music, is an examination of the value of Classical Music. The following questions need to be answered by the enthusiast of any art form:

- ❖ What do I get for my money or time investment?
- ❖ What's in it for me?
- ❖ What's the profit?

I have to get more out of it than I put into it. I think that I do, and this whole book is an explanation of just what I do get out of it. It's not a matter of money, for the profit is the difference between the expenditure of my time in listening to the music, as well as the money expended on it, and what takes place inside me. What I get is so great, that it's cheap at any price. I can't set a valuation to it, but I do declare that it is valuable.

My grandchildren, to whom this book is dedicated, are too young to have a large enough frame of reference to understand everything I'm saying and advocating here, but one day they will, and I hope, then, that they'll read Grandpa's book and make a profit of their own on it. Music has contributed to the formation of my personality, and I believe it could do so for them, too.

1. How I Started Down This Road

I am not a professional musician. By vocation, I have been a preacher for the majority of my adult life. For an interval of ten years, I worked as an office administrator in the business world. I can sing and play the piano, though not on a virtuoso level. My mother's aim in getting me lessons was that I would be able to play out of the hymn book. My piano teacher thought I would be the next Van Cliburn. He had burst onto the musical world the year before I started taking piano lessons. I think I stayed closer to my mother's vision, but there is a little of the showman in my playing beyond simply hitting the notes out of the hymn book. Most of what I like in Classical Music I couldn't play or sing, but I love it.

During my ministry years, I did a message entitled, "Can I Tell You Who I Am?" Both of the times I did this, my goal was to reveal to the members of my congregations who their preacher was as a person and not merely as a ministry "professional". My musical preferences were a significant part of these presentations.

I don't feel it was unusual or inappropriate to take a break for one Sunday to give a little insight into the culture of my heart. I've heard a lot of preachers expound at length their love of a particular baseball team or some other sporting activity. I've never been a sports person, but I have shared illustrations that have come to me through the arts. They are a part of me, but they are not autonomous. My faith is to connected with the totality of my life and culture.

It's not surprising that as a preacher and a Christian I would like Christian kinds of music and the oft time fellow-travelers in the Country field along with Elvis. But Classical Music, the realm of the high brow cerebral elites? I actually came to it long before I discovered Southern Gospel Music.

They say that "The Journey of a Thousand Miles begins with a single step." In my case, it took three steps, but, then, I think I've covered a lot more than a thousand miles since taking these three steps.

You don't have to "grow up with" music or any other art form to love it. You can discover it for yourself.

I didn't grow up in a home with Classical Music. My folks didn't have what could be called a record collection or listen to any kind of music on the radio that I can remember. The music we had in my home was either little kid records or piano music and hymn books. I remember a few recordings of some light classics we had, but I don't think I'd have ever come to a love for Classical Music from those. There were three influences, all outside my home, which started me down this road.

I had piano lessons from the time I was in the third grade in 1959, but it was Miss Juanita Wolff, a few years later, who probably first introduced me to Classical Music from the viewpoint of being a listening consumer of the music.

Miss Wolff was a music teacher in the elementary system in Portland, Oregon. She covered a circuit of schools and would come to us at William Clark Elementary School one or two days a week.

Outside the classroom, she had a program on the local educational radio station called "Fun With Music". I had heard about it, but I don't remember ever actually hearing it. It was either not on at a time I could hear it or else the teachers I had didn't choose to use it was a part of their classroom curriculum. I have a feeling, though, that some of the things she taught us were what had been previously explored over the airwaves.

I learned basics about writing notation from her. I knew how to read music from my piano lessons, but she taught how to write the notes and other musical features such as the clefs and dynamic markings. We didn't do any composition, but it was a foundation which was added to by an extra credit short term informal class I participated in when I was in high school which formed the totality of my training in composition.

She gave basic teaching on types of music also. I first learned of the categories of sacred and secular from her. That may be the beginning of my schematic. In her choir, she took us beyond the children's songs and show hits of the day. Yes, we did "Supercalifragilisticexpialidocious", but we also did "Dona Nobis Pacem". She was not afraid to teach us the Latin pronunciations and do a song with some real history to it. You could do that in the public schools in those days. No one regarded it as an imposition of belief or intrusion of religion. It was simply exposure to music.

As a part of music class, she also played some classical recordings. She was the one who introduced me to "The Grand Canyon Suite" by Ferde Grofe. She played one movement each week until we got through the whole thing. Later on, I borrowed a recording of the suite from my friend, Chuck Keller, so I could hear the complete work in its own context.

What Miss Wolff did was to introduce us to something accessible to our age and interest level. Program music is probably a better place to start with children than absolute music is. They can relate to the pictures conjured up by the sound world. Being a boy, I was most intrigued by the natural violence of the Cloudburst movement. The music made things happen. It was not just a succession of sounds, but a sound world. Miss Wolff showed me that music could speak to me, and that it could have a place inside my life.

Other teachers played Classical Music from time to time in the classroom. One of them did so when we were doing art one day. We listened to the music and drew a picture of what it inspired in us. I don't think my picture was any good, but I enjoyed the music.

That teacher was trying to expand our

schematic to show how an audio medium could have an impact on the visual arts. This was a bridge between the world of sound and sight. The two are interconnected.

On a cultural level, the movies increased their impact dramatically with the addition of sound. It wasn't just hearing the voices, but the enhancement which the musical soundtrack provided. Max Steiner, in 1933, was first to synchronized the music with the action for dramatic effect. A total experience was born with "King Kong".

Miss Wolff died very suddenly in her 40s, so her influence didn't extend beyond my grade school years, but I still remember her energy and enthusiasm. I don't know how far her personal schematic extended or if she would have liked everything I have come to like, but she would have liked my liking it. She loved music.

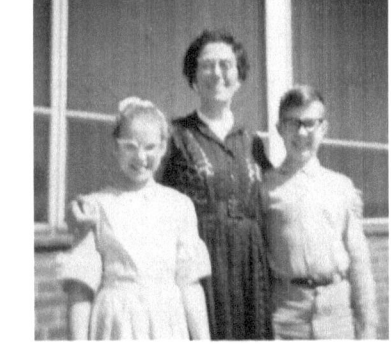

Miss Wolff with my sister, Donae Sue, and I
27 May 1963

Chuck Keller was about 7 years older than me, but he was the older brother I never had who mentored me in many ways. I got to know him because I went to his house for a Neighborhood Bible Club which his mother led. He especially encouraged my participation in the arts.

I don't know how he connected up with me in the area of music, but I can still remember listening to Rachmaninov's second symphony for the first time at his house. He had a reel to reel tape player and had recorded it off the radio a night or two before I had come over for a visit. He suggested that I might like to listen to it. The first five minutes of the piece had a weight and drama unlike anything I had ever heard before.

This was not kid's music or popular music like Grofe's or even the music track of a movie. It was music performing powerfully on its own. In some ways, the rest of the symphony never matched the power of those first minutes. Over the years, I've bought several recordings of the piece, first on lp, then on cd. I still feel that way about it, and I still love it. This is one of the few pieces which has a definite niche in my history.

I listened to other music at Chuck's. He had a commercially produced reel to reel tape of Beethoven's Missa Solemnis that was the beginning of my love of sacred choral music.

As a result of hearing this music at his home, I wanted to hear it in my own. Since it was broadcast on FM in our area, and we didn't have an FM radio in our home, I took my first earnings from lawn mowing and bought an AM/FM radio. It was just a little monaural player, but I could access the world of Classical Music. It was only broadcast on two stations in Portland, and neither one of them was exclusively devoted to music, but I would listen many nights to the programs all the way through. One time, when I was in high school, the Philadelphia Orchestra under Eugene Ormandy came to Portland. I couldn't go to hear them in person, but the performance was broadcast, and I was thrilled. I can remember hearing them play the second Daphnis and Chloe suite by Ravel. In those days, everything was new, but it was all being catalogued into my memory as something to purchase later on when I had the capability of doing so.

In Chuck, I found the power of mentoring and personal involvement. This was not just a classroom training session, but one person affecting another. Chuck also encouraged me in my early love of Shakespeare and the drama. The personal element will do what the classroom cannot always accomplish, and it will stay with a person longer.

Chuck was a strong Christian, and he showed me that Christianity and the arts are not exclusive of one another. While he didn't teach me any of the specifics set down in this book, he gave me the foundation for understanding the spirituality, transport and threshold of music. By just enjoying a thing, you receive more than you could ever get by willfully studying and taming it into a paper or a test answer. I'm not denigrating music education, but boosting music love. Education is only a means to knowledge. You are the end of education.

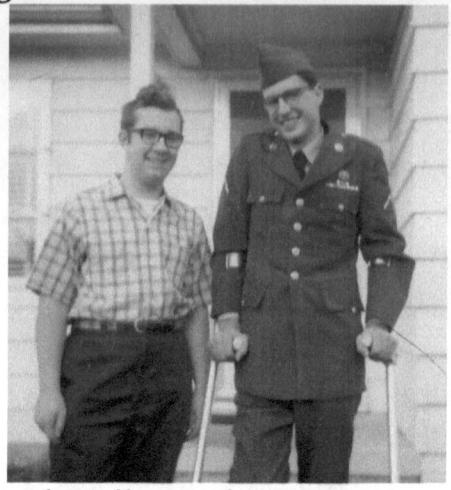

Chuck Keller and I, 1 January 1968
Chuck was recovering from wounds received in
Vietnam at the time of this picture

The third stream came from television. It was the Leonard Bernstein Young Person's Concerts. I don't know how or when I started watching those, but it was some time during my grade school years. I do know that I did it on my own and not as a school assignment.

There were a few other isolated Classical Music programs I can remember seeing on television, some recommended by teachers, others just discovered on my own. The most memorable was Stravinsky's "The Flood". I wish that broadcast from the early 1960s was available on dvd; it was very hard to track down even an audio recording of that piece. Then, there were Horowitz and Rubinstein in separate concert programs. I was particularly interested in Horowitz's pedal work and Rubinstein's finger warm ups back stage. I think I use the pedals when I play the piano more than I would because of seeing Horowitz do it. These were isolated inputs. It was Bernstein's concerts which were the steady diet.

Bernstein, the teacher I chose for myself, provided me with a real education. I can remember the specifically themed programs on subjects such as the sonata form, jazz music and the then new electronic music featuring a Moog Synthesizer which was wheeled out onto the stage. I first heard the music of Ives and Shostakovich on these programs. Beyond that, I don't remember many specifics on pieces performed. It was more the creation of an appetite for the music that came out of these programs. I was the only one in our house who watched them, so when no one was looking, I would get in front of the television set and conduct along with Leonard.

He began with his own intense love for the music which he communicated to those in the viewing audience. I didn't know at the time about his own compositions. I have since acquired all of his symphonies and many other works on cd. He was important as a communicator of the music. When he retired from the series after I was out of college, it didn't seem the same to see Michael Tilson Thomas presenting the programs. He was knowledgeable, but he didn't have the engaging personality Bernstein had projected which had drawn me to the music.

The Portland Symphony Orchestra had young people's concerts which I was actually able to attend but they didn't have the place in my heart that the Bernstein broadcasts did. This was one time where television seemed the greater reality.

Leonard Bernstein showed that music is on our side. It is not trying to attack us; it is for us. It is not a burden; it is a pleasure. You can't love something which you think is against you or which you are mandated to love without a choice.

I became so interested in this music that I would take the time to paw through every lp in bins of clearance albums to find the one classical album hidden in their midst. It was a hit and miss collection method, but many which I found were standard works.

Among the first lps I acquired were: Tchaikovsky's 1812 Overture, Brahms' 1st symphony, Schubert's 3rd symphony, Tchaikovsky's 1st piano concerto, Haydn's 44th symphony (and many others of his), and Beethoven's 9th symphony. I can still remember the day I got the Beethoven 9. It was the first regular priced album I ever bought, although it was from the RCA budget line. My folks had wondered if I would be wasting my money in finding out that it was something I didn't really like. I took an immediate liking to it. I still listen to all these pieces I started out with.

When I graduated from high school, I spent most of my graduation gift money on getting a reel to reel recorder so I could record off the FM station as Chuck had done. They expected that you would do that, then, and on one program, the announcer would tell ahead of time the duration of a featured piece so that you could "add it to your tape library". The tape player has long gone, along with those tapes, but much of the music I first got off the radio has stayed with me and was eventually replaced by lps, and then the lps by cassettes, and then the cassettes by cds.

Miss Wolff opened the door, Chuck showed me what was inside, and Leonard helped me to make some sense of it and to begin to schematicize it. All three streams into my Classical Music consciousness were personal. They all valued the music themselves. They were not just trying to get me interested in it for some ulterior motive, but they saw a benefit which would come to me.

Music is intensely personal. Even though, in the early days of the Gregorian Chants, all personal elements were missing as was true in almost all the arts then, now it's always personal. We can see that clearly in popular music forms. It is just as true here. In a world of increasing impersonality, we are well reminded that we are persons designed for sharing with other persons.

2. The Appeal Of Music

There are clear cut reasons why we enjoy music. They lie inside us as well as in the nature of the music itself. In a question of which came first, the love of it or the music itself, I'd have to give the music an edge, at least in terms of chronological priority, but both factors are involved in the end result.

In a sense, all love, but the love of God for us, is reactionary. We love God because He first loved us. We love people who are there. We love doing things in a world which already exists. We can create songs or pieces, but no one can create music. It existed from the beginning.

God told Job that the morning stars sang together at the time of creation (Job 38:7). Music as a principle precedes our creation and consumption of it. Composers or songwriters start with the words and notes and music forms which are there. Even anti-forms, such as atonalism or serialism, use the same notes and signatures which are used in other music.

Music is intrinsically valuable. It is the expression of the spirit of a composer and of the musicians performing the work. Music "works" because there is inside us something which it appeals to. Music is both objective and subjective, often all at the same time, although it can appeal to us from the two extremes of the spectrum.

Music can be categorized in many ways.

Some have classified it as either being absolute music or programmatic music. Those are valid categories, for everything would fit into one or the other of them. That way of dealing with music speaks of the division among the groupings from the viewpoint of the intention of the composer. I prefer to speak of it from the viewpoint of the listener.

I saw this in a single night at the Hollywood Bowl in the late 90s. They had billed it as a world gospel night, although one of the groups was not Christian, but Moslem. What struck me that night was the way that the first two groups fit into the cerebral camp, and the last two into the emotional. Everything that was there was music. Everyone in the audience was reached by one of the types, but not every one was attuned to everything.

And, that's all right. There's nothing that says we have to all like the same thing. In fact, having to like the same thing that others like is probably the biggest stumbling block to learning to love music. No one wants to be just one more of the same. So, we'll not do it. I'll like what I like, and you can like what you like, and none of us will look down on the other for his or her preferences.

How would you describe your likes on the basis of these two headings, cerebral and emotional? I'll start with some examples which everyone who has even the slightest inkling of what Classical Music is has heard or heard of, with one possible exception.

Cerebral movements and composers would include such as Gregorian Chant, Bach, Mozart and many modern composers such as Steve Reich.

Emotional music would include most of the Romantics, patriotic music by composers such as Sousa and Elgar, along with light music such as that of the Strauss family.

There are midpoints also, including both elements. Chief among them is Haydn. I both think about and feel his music.

As far as I know, up to this time, there has been no discovery of notational systems for most ancient music. Some of it has been described, but there is not a book you can go to which will give the notes in terms of pitch and time as our modern systems do from which the music could be performed. The book of Psalms in the Bible is only a book of lyrics. It gives references to melodies in some of the superscriptions, but we do not know what those were. The beginning, in Western circles, at least, of what has come down to us of music is the chant.

Up until the release of the best selling "Chant" cd in 1994, Gregorian chant was regarded as either historical oddity or as something belonging to the realm of the very specialized listener. I doubt if, by 1994, there were even any Roman Catholic churches at which Gregorian chant was being performed on a weekly basis in any kind of worship setting, although from the fact that the monks recorded these pieces, we can deduce that *they* were still using or at least performing them.

Then, came the New Age which embraced the Gregorian Chant. Not being a New Age advocate, I cannot speak of the uses to which they put the music in their meditation, but they did do us a great service by bringing it back into the mainstream. It not only brought us the various recording monks, but also paved the way for the angelically sublime Anonymous 4.

I don't understand Latin, so it is not the words of the chant which speak to me. I'm not a Roman Catholic, so the doctrines of Mary and the other elements of the Catholic liturgy do not speak to me. But, the music speaks inside me.

There is a beauty in the single line of the melody which is unparalleled in the rest of the Classical repertoire. It is so simple, yet it plunges deep inside a person. That is probably why non-Christian people would want to use this music. It has an understanding inside itself. It is a thing to evoke astonishment.

No one can hear this music and not operate on a thought level. We won't be tapping our feet or swaying to the rhythm as we put the cd into our player. When we listen to it, our heart beat doesn't race any faster than it did before. We're not roused as we would be by a Sousa March, but our thoughts are stirred. I say we, and although I think this is a universal experience with regard to chant, the only one I can testify of is myself.

This music appeals to consciousness. It

makes me wake up so as to hear it. I can drift off from some light music, but not this. Even if it does seem to be all the same, for me, it is nothing I could go to sleep by. I would always be following it with my mind.

Bach is the greatest in almost everything cerebral. He did not live in an era given over to emotion in music as would later be the case in the 19th century. It could be that that is why his children and others at the end of his life regarded him as passé. They were entering into a new realm of living outside the heart, but Bach was committed to living by the heart. His music directed the heart through its appeal to the head.

You can't get away from Bach. We'll come to him again and again. When we acclaim him, we are in company with the great composers such as Beethoven, Mozart and Mendelssohn, who all paid him the highest honors.

In popular culture, Mozart is coupled with increasing brain power, but to me it is Bach. I can't prove it on a quantitative basis, but I think it. Bach is precision and order. His exercise pieces are totally given over to these. No one can hear the Well Tempered Clavier, and not immediately understand the nature of musical organization. We also experience it all of his other works.

Bach's music was made to fit, not just a regional or momentary mold, but the world as a whole. He signed his works SDG – Soli Deo Gloria. By composing, he declared that Glory was God's alone. Even though there was glory in his music, it came from and extended back to God. He knew this, not as an emotional experience, but as an abiding principle of body, soul and spirit. The Mind of God is the framework for the music of Bach. It can be explained no other way. Even secular works, such as the Coffee Cantata, fit into that Mind, for it is one which encompasses everything.

Now, I wasn't bashing Mozart a few paragraphs ago when I put Bach ahead of him. I have a big collection of Mozart cds. We may not tap our toes or clap our hands to Mozart's music, and no one feels an irresistible impulse today to get up and dance to his minuets, but we do follow the pace and melody which constitute his greatness. I have nothing but respect for Mozart's music. It, too, is precision and order, but it is the order of the mind of Mozart and not the Mind of God. He was a genius, but even a genius can't be the framework for everything.

This may be the fundamental difference between the music of Bach and Mozart: we will always feel drawn to God by Bach, for God never changes, but we will not always be drawn to the concerns of Mozart by Mozart, because his world has changed and given way to many others in the interim between his day and ours. Of course, here I'm impinging on the element of universality as well as promoting my own schematic.

I will pass by many others as examples to get to one which is contemporary to the time of writing this book, Steve Reich. I would have included another name with his, but just a few months before I began work on this book, we lost a monumental contemporary. Elliott Carted died, so I can no longer speak of him as contemporary. Now, his corpus is fixed and will not develop any more. Posthumously published works may change it's totality and even show a new direction, but once they all come to light, there will be no more change. The living composer is always subject to growth and change.

Steve Reich and the entire Minimalist movement (although I'm not sure everything Reich has done could be said to be minimalist) are extreme examples of cerebralism in modern times. I don't say they are the farthest cerebralism could go, but they are the farthest I've gone. Listening to tape music, sometimes random sounds, and endless repetitions with slight variations, takes me back to the realm of chant. It's not the same, but it feels, to use a non-cerebral word, like it. A few resources are made to do a lot of work. It is a work which appeals to the head almost exclusively.

My first response to music at this end of the spectrum is to think about it. It doesn't mean that I won't have feelings about the various merits of these pieces, but that they are not the primary event in experiencing such music.

It always takes me a little while to get used to something along this line, but, once my schematic is expanded to include it, I am nourished. It does something deep inside me. I don't always know what that something is, but I know it has occurred. It opens the door to examination and thought. It's not about analyzing the music itself, but that I am prone to think while I'm hearing it or to reflect after it's finished. Absolute music is in sync with concrete thinking. The appeal to my mind has been made.

The emotional appeal employs more of the senses and seeks to arouse us rather than to instigate thoughts within us. It sets our feet tapping and our imagination soaring, but usually it doesn't focus our attention on ourselves. It focuses us on our feelings. Much programmatic music fits this category as well as what we would call the "light classics".

Emotionally charged music really came into its own with the Romantics. Beethoven is usually credited with being the one who started the ball rolling. I don't know who can be specifically credited with beginning Romanticism, but you can see his journey toward it beginning with the progression from the first symphony, which doesn't seem that much removed from the worlds of Haydn and Mozart, to the total movement of the ninth in which the world was changed by his genius. The music of emotion was carried even further by those who followed, such as Berlioz, Liszt, Chopin, Tchaikovsky and the Russians.

The Romantics do not seem to have been interested in forms as the earlier composers of the

Baroque and Classical eras were. Even if they did some work in that manner, it is not what has come down to us as their works of importance. I've never come across any Toccatas by Strauss or Tchaikovsky. If they did write them, they haven't been promoted to the music loving public. Strauss moved the dancers' feet and bodies. Tchaikovsky moved the entire soul of a nation with his symphonies and 1812 Overture.

Something stirs deep down inside when we hear this music. Leroy Anderson's "Sleigh Ride" puts us on the snow, every time we hear it. The exceptional thing about it is that after the ride, no one catches a cold, but we feel the sense of exhilaration which we imagine, even if it is not so, goes with such an excursion.

Midway between the two approaches are my favorites, Haydn and Vivaldi. Neither are programmatic as we think of that approach in terms of the Romantic era, nor do they have the orchestral colorations the Romantics employed, but they are far beyond the realm of thinking alone.

Both composers are intensely bright. Both lift me up. Haydn may have participated in the Sturm und Drang movement for a time, though I've read some liner notes which seem to question that, but it was a movement which aroused rather than depressed. We often relate to negative emotions more readily than to positive ones. As he shaped the symphony and string quartet to what they are today, Haydn carried us from the average that others were doing for their patrons to an enduring, still existent, sublime. He encouraged life from the inside out.

Vivaldi gave ideas of the seasons in his most well known series of compositions, but they were not impressions such as might have been given by Debussy or Ravel had they been the ones to write the seasonal standard. He attaches names to the pieces, but leaves our hearts free to soar in all the seasons.

I would also put some more modern composers such as Mahler, Bruckner, and, even surprisingly, Ives in the middle category. The first two listed expand on the work of Haydn, taking us both internally and externally to a greater degree of emotional depth. Ives speaks to me through his use of hymn tunes and other familiar melodies which are engraved on my heart from the time before I knew there was such a thing as Classical Music. I can't quite relax with him as I would with a Leroy Anderson piece, but at the same time, I'm not totally over in the cerebral camp with the Minimalists when I hear him, either.

To illustrate the differences between cerebral, emotional and midway music, I will offer three different pieces, all dealing with the same subject, in this case insects. I like all of these pieces, but each one reaches me in a different way.
Cerebral: George Crumb's "Night Of The Electric Insects" which begins his larger work, "Black Angels (Images I) For Electronic String Quartet" puts the

relationship with insects on a purely intellectual level. These are not real insects, but rather disturbing sounds which represent them. We have an abstract representation. Their activity is transferred to us where it races around inside our brains.

Emotional: Albert Roussel's "Spider's Feast" was a work I first heard on a record I checked out from the Portland library. There were other programmatic pieces on it, as well, but this is the one which struck such a chord in me that years later I spent a long time, on the basis of only a few hearings in the 1960s, looking for a recording of the piece before I found one. It doesn't exactly give me a feeling of rapacity, but of nature coming to life and interacting in its various parts.

Midway: Kalevi Aho's Symphony No. 7 "Insect Symphony" lies somewhere between the two. It has the emotional movement of Roussel with the edge of Crumb. I think I bought it because I was expecting a second helping of Roussel, but then you can't expect anyone to give you more of what someone else gave you. Each has his or her own to give.

Everyone can divide up the appeal of music on his own categorical bases, but putting it into camps, such as I've done, is the beginning of forming a schematic. That helps me to be able to love the music by being able to understand where it fits inside me. For example, I'm not expecting cerebral music to move me, so I can experience it for what it is. I can use it when I want to have the pot of my thinking stirred by something outside myself.

We need more than one kind of music, just like we need both knowledge and feeling in every day life. Classical Music provides these two extremes in a way that popular music does not. I love Southern Gospel, and I even wrote a book about it called <u>What Makes It Southern</u>, but, by way of comparison, it's pretty much what it is. It appeals to the spirit, but it does so openly through the words and the message behind them.

Here, we will not be defining Classical Music, but looking at what it does for us. I'm not saying that one is better than the other; they are just different. This has something more because we are something more. A product of chance could not be moved to both think and feel by a single medium. We are more than chance, and we can move on more than one matrix.

3.   The Message Of Music

What is it that music is saying? Does it have an agenda, or do we create one for it by our listening? Can we learn it's language?

The message of music isn't like the Lost Dutchman Mine, something once seen and then lost forever. It's ultimately the meaning which is brought out of our hearts and minds when we hear it. This is where the two appeals reach us and where we go to work on what we have heard.

Students are often taught to "hear" things in music, to determine its structure and form, rather than to hear the music in and with their hearts. Life is more than structure or we would all just be skeletons. The message comes to life when it comes to life in our hearts. Listening doesn't happen to us; it's something we do.

This doesn't mean that the composer didn't have a message in mind when a piece was written. Ferde Grofe proclaimed very plainly what the Grand Canyon Suite was about in both the title of the work as a whole and in the titles of the five movements. I've never been to the Grand Canyon, but this music does more than evoke a place I've never been to. It raises up a feel for the qualities found in that place which I can relate to out of the sound world created by the piece.

Whenever music is performed, two parallel universes intersect. To differentiate and describe them is almost as difficult as it was for the square to explain the sphere he had encountered to the other two dimensional geometric figures in the classic book Flatland. Both are there. The composer may have never intended or seen what arises in me, but, even if it is different than what he intended, both his message sent and my message received or perceived are valid and full of meaning. Music is not like language in which a specific message must be translated accurately. It is almost a medium beyond required meaning which gives meaning.

The first meaning is formed by the intention of the composer. The other is what I, the listener, make of it. A conductor or soloist will need to know the first in order to be authentic in performance, but I don't always need to understand the writer's intentions or the historical background leading to a particular composition in order to receive it.

We'll take it as an axiom that all music has a primary meaning which is given it in its creation and other meanings which are or can be given it by our hearing.

Even if we get the intended meaning wrong, there is still something for us in the music. Disney showed that when his studio translated music into animation in "Fantasia". Bach's notes turned into rhythmic images. Stravinsky's primitive ballet became an evolutionary statement. (I don't agree with the evolution, but, then, I have my own meaning attached to the music which is not confined to a pagan exercise which the ballet purports to depict, but which is more of a general enthusiasm for life.) The well known "Dance of The Hours" became the comic relief. The Disney people did not mar the music or do injustice to it by their accompanying animated figures. They merely allowed their artists to interpret its message in their world.

Music can speak of a composer's ultimate beliefs. No one was ever mistaken about Bach's supreme belief in God. On the other hand, the chance music of John Cage pictured a completely different kind of world view. Music is not exclusively about theology or philosophy, though. It's about the heart.

Music always makes me think and feel. I listen almost all the time I am home or in the car. It is there in the background, and it moves through me. As I'm typing the rough draft of this chapter, I have Stravinsky on in the background. It's the more contemplative section of the "Nightingale" opera. I'm not even sure what the language is, but I don't need to know the words. It's the movement of the music that speaks to me. I understand the ebb and flow of relationships and activity in it.

I may not always think a particular thought about the music itself when I'm hearing it, but the music can be a catalyst to my thinking. Music kicks up the thought level. There are people who are not be attuned to music, but I am. Because I have listened for so many years, I am able to work hand in hand with what I hear, rather than being stopped in my tracks by it.

I see when I hear. I see emotions moving in the world around me and in myself. Sometimes they are deliberately aroused; other times they sneak in unawares. They are expressed, communicated and validated by music. All Americans sit or stand a little more intensely when they hear a Sousa march or a rendition of one of our national songs. It could be regarded as a sort of Jingoism, but it is a genuine sentiment.

At times, music rouses us to rage. Some music was composed with the aim of disturbing. We may not be aware of what the specific agenda of disturbance is, but the music shouts that nothing which occurs is neutral. Here are things to be resisted or at least be made aware of.

Other times, music speaks of peace. Some instruments, such as the flute or harp, especially give this message, although I've also heard those instruments in combative modes, also.

Music makes strong declarations. It speaks of how the composer or performers feel about the world. It speaks of how the world actually is. It speaks of how we wish it would be. It speaks of what it finds inside me.

Music not only speaks of experience, but, at times, provides it. It allows me to experience what I might never experience in the flesh. Villa Lobos' little train has taken more people on an excursion than any real locomotive ever did. Even in our day, in which very few people have traveled by train, there is a romance about that little train.

Music means that I can receive the world where I am, without having to go to every part of it. It means that I can go through the worst emotions and be safe. No matter how dark the piece, when it is done, I am free to move on. I do not have to be bound by its meaning. When I experience a real world catastrophe, I am not so free. We lived in Los Angeles county during the Rodney King riots, and no one was free of them while they lasted.

Freedom is one of the aspects and meanings of music. One is freed from having to do everything to experience it. One is freed from the limitations of body or space or technology or possibility. It doesn't seem as though anyone will set foot on Mars in my lifetime due to lack of funding in that direction, but every time I hear Holst's Mars, I experience the planet without a rocket. I also think of the news, because the local public station I listened to when I was first listening to this music played a snippet of that movement at the beginning of each news broadcast. The music tells me that something is coming which is of significance.

Music is a connection, not only to things outside of us, but between things inside us. It is a balancing force, a connective force, a building force. Whenever we connect two things together, which were apart before, we are building. Music gives meaning to our thoughts. It can declare them to be important or feasible. It can certify that they need to be communicated.

Ultimately, I'm not talking about finding meaning, but about making meaning, and it is not a meaning for the music itself as much as it is a meaning for ourselves. This is something we have to do every day. Classical Music is a blessing because there are occasions on which it quickens or enables that meaning process and fits it into life.

One of the messages of music is that we are defined by our music. You are not a bit of cosmic dust. You mean something. Your life, your inner person, your relationships, your thoughts, your viewpoints, all have meaning. You are not just a cipher to be decoded or dispensed with. Classical Music may help you to express or bring about understanding of your meaning. It is not the only medium which does that, but it does it extremely well.

What the notes do to us is important because we are important recipients of the total music. The notes make it music, the music makes it us.

4. Universality

I can explore any piece of Classical Music without having to learn anything about it ahead of time. Granted, I can have an enhanced understanding by knowing musical forms and the cultural and historical backgrounds to the music, but those are not obligatory requisites to experience. Classical Music is universally accessible. It's not always that way in other arts.

I like literature as well as music. In order to read <u>War And Peace</u>, a book which I have read three times, I need a translator since I will probably never learn to read Russian. On the other hand, from the first time I heard Tchaikovsky, I knew him. No interpreter had to come between us. He spoke directly to my heart.

No other art form requires such little preparation for experience. You just listen. Anyone can listen to anything and get something out of it. Even if you don't like it, your very aversion to the sound world you are rejecting says something about you. We don't all have to like everything in music, but we can all get something from anything.

Music transcends both its original eras and cultures in bringing people together. It probably would not have had much opportunity to do so in the past because of the great distances which kept those at the court of Esterhazy from hearing the melodies of Japan. Still, John Field traveled far from his native Ireland to have his music consumed so greatly in Russia that Leo Tolstoy would mention the composer by name in <u>War And Peace</u>. It was a one way importation of the Irish composer to Russia, but I believe that if the distance factor had not been involved, the conversation would have been two way between Ireland and Russia as it is capable of being so today.

Music may express someone else's world. When I hear it, I walk in that world. Neither the visual arts nor literature can do that with as great ease for me.

It doesn't do it for me alone. It unites me with others. All music connects. Some music brings us together on the basis or our emotions or impulses. Other music expresses an exclusive culture which doesn't want understanding by outsiders, but which can always be known and identified by them. Identification is a form of understanding, and it is not to be denigrated.

Classical Music unites hearts in a way that other music does not. It does not insist on being generational or provincial, even when it is. By the very fact of its performance, it reaches out to the entire world. I have no idea about the exact location of the Hardanger region, but I don't need to know that when I hear Gierr Tveitt's Hardanger Suites and Folk-Tunes. I rejoice in the music as I hear it. The Hardanger region has come to me.

No composer or performer would be happy to set limits on the reception of what they do. They want people who would not be able to converse with them in their native tongue to cheer together with them in their music. To do music is to engage in universality.

Music is the only language which doesn't need to be interpreted. Everyone can listen to it and decide what to like and what to leave behind for someone else to like. We each have our own circle, but all the circles are entwined together. Eventually every circle can be connected to every other circle. Somewhere there is a point of connection for everyone who engages in the world of Classical Music. This can be true in the entire world of life, too. We are all constituent parts of creation, bound together by our being creatures.

In the final analysis, music asserts our identities as persons. You can't be a nihilist and do music. Music implies meaning, in the composer, in the performer, in the listener. It implies human connection. It implies heart. While we do not all have the same tastes, we all have hearts, and there is hardly a person living who can hear who is not moved by some kind of music. It is one of the few universal experiences of mankind.

Music gives us a common experience which does not require words. It reaches our hearts directly through our ears. Whatever speaks to a heart, speaks to a person. We are persons.

5.   Diversity

It's strange that between universality and unity should come diversity. It would appear as though those three concepts could not mix or have any relationship to one another, but we need both something to unite to and the ability to go our own way when we'd like to. We get both in classical music.

America is not a single culture any longer, if it ever was. The melting pot which was made so much of in my childhood is no longer mentioned by anyone. We are not expected to melt into one another. We have come to a state of pluralism. There is no longer one single culture which is the standard in which all others will be grafted. The cultures of generation, race, region and specific interests are all flourishing at the same time side by side without impinging on one another.

Classical music is not a succession of periods, but a lot of streams meandering hither and yon in different directions with different rates of flow and even different destinations all at the same time. There's never been a time when someone could state that the whole world is "HERE" in music. Historically, we can often look back and label what appears to be the prevalent elements of cohesiveness to a period, but while we're living in our own period, it's not always so easy to do that. In fact, it's only long after a period is over that anyone knows it was an identifiable era of culture.

Music offers something to everyone, thus it is universal, but the fact that everyone can be served by it shows that it is diverse.

The differences are all right. We don't have to all be alike. We never did.

The arts are no longer homogenized. I don't believe they ever were, but there was a time in which everyone seemed to do everything together except for a few fringe folks that nobody cared about. Culture appeared to be monolithic. Not so any longer.

I don't believe there will ever be another <u>Gone With The Wind</u> which everyone will read and then go see on the screen. There will never be another Bing Crosby which everyone will listen to. Even as late as the mid 1970s, the claim was made and substantiated that the voice of Bing Crosby had been heard by more people than the voice of any other person in history. That was still true well into the careers of Frank Sinatra and Elvis Presley. We used to have a minimum of three television networks which covered the field, but with satellite, cable and dvds even they have lost their solidarity with the nation.

Classical music is operating in the same way, but it continues to maintain its past as the same time as it celebrates its present. It is diverse and distinct on the contemporary rim of the wheel. Every time I get a new BBC Music Magazine I see more and more names I've never heard of. Things are growing farther apart the further the spokes go out, but at the same time the hub is still the standards of Bach, Beethoven and Brahms (my piano teacher's Three B's) and the like. The concerts and record catalogues are more full of them than ever. Beethoven's 9th will always get an audience. I don't think it can be over-recorded. It's not that it's safe to perform or endorse, but it speaks with just as much power as it ever did and everybody who can do it wants to do it.

There is enough for everyone to have something of his own. The overall umbrella can cover a lot of ground. It also means that some things can come along that don't necessarily become main stream, but which are still valuable in and of themselves. Twelve Tone never took over, but people still listen to it. The electronic music of the 60s is about the farthest out stuff I've heard, other than John Cage's piece using cactus as an instrument. I can dip into it from time to time, even though it's not mainstream, so I'm glad it's there. It gives an alternative at times to find a fresh viewpoint on what I do like.

At times there have been musical styles and genres which have been defining in their era. Thus we had chant, the concertos of Vivaldi, the symphonies of Haydn, the whole oeuvre of Beethoven. They have been pace setters, but not everything has to be a pace setter. It just has to be what it is so that those who like it can come and receive something. The others don't have to run it down. They can just hear what they like – or that's how it should be.

The diverse allows us to each be ourselves without damaging others. I don't have to like what you like; you don't have to like what I like. Instead of finding a pizza that everyone will like the toppings of (a dilemma we faced with three grandchildren and three adults a while back) and resorting to wrangling and strife even among the adults, each one of us gets our own. The downside is that it's more expensive and we have lost the common fellowship of all eating from the same pie, but it allows us to sit together in peace.

If everyone is diverse, then we have a connection for we are all diverse together. There's no need for my satisfaction to hinder your enjoyment. We can each take pleasure in what we like. To go back to the pizza illustration, it's a way to stay at the table without having to eat what we don't like. This is why we can love the music. We are no longer being forced to conform, but we are allowed free choice. With that we can live with others and really live ourselves.

6.   Unity

For a long time I have felt that we have come full circle. Modern music has almost returned to early music like the ouroboros. The mouth which is creating the current music has reached around and taken hold of the known tail which is the farthest removed from the present. We are seeing two ends of the same creature.

Take a look at early music such as chant or Hildegard. Then, put it side by side with some of our contemporaries such as Stravinsky, Part and Penderecki. The modern composers are obviously modern. No one would mistake their work for an ancient piece recently rediscovered, but there is an affinity of sparseness, of taking some small atom of sound and building a great bridge out of it. It is as though we passed through the complications of polyphony, the baroque, the Romantics and the modern to come back to the starting point and begin creating music anew. This is one example which shows the unity of music.

Music is more like a circle than a line or geometric figure. It does not follow a straight time line of development and divestiture. It is bound up in many things and binds many together. A straight line goes from point A to point B, but a circle does away with points. Wherever you are at on the circle is point A. Wherever you go is point A. You can go all the way around and come back and it will not be another letter.

The identity of Classical Music remains a whole. It may contain multiple personalities and movements and ages, but it is one being. The circle is always a circle. Over time, it simply grows to be a larger circle, but it never becomes a square or a trapezoid. This fits with the concept of spirituality, for we start in God and always end in Him unless we get out of the circle.

We live in an age of fracture. We are fractured in ourselves and from one another and our technologies. We tear things down to their smallest possible components, and then try to make a picture which makes sense. As with Pointillism and the television set, you need to step back for the perspective which will enable you to perceive the picture.

Musically, we do that by looking at as much of the musical spectrum as we can. If we only know one small era or genre, we will never "see the picture". No one may notice the countryside in the background of the Mona Lisa, but if all there was to the painting was a smile, it would hardly be appealing.

To love something, we have be take it as a unit. Parts presuppose a whole. It is the whole which we love, even if we don't like every component. By acknowledging the genres we are not fond of as valid, we are able to acknowledge others for being valid even when they are unlike us. That is one of the premier qualities of love.

Even modern music's dissonance testifies to

the existence of the conventional by being regarded as dissonant. It's interesting, though, but I don't think I've ever heard anyone speak of any music as being sonant or having sonance. Those are real words, but they are not used to positively describe anything in the way dissonance, their antonym, is used to denigrate.

It is time to start thinking of sonance. In the world of Classical Music, sonance is more than a sound or a tune. It is a complete integration and compatibility within a piece and within all surrounding music.

Music is not static. Dissonance can become sonant. I first heard "The Rite Of Spring" about 50 years after its riot provoking premiere. By that time, it had been integrated into the musical scene as a whole, and the dissonance was not extremely noticeable in light of what had come after it. It could be that yesterday's dissonance is simply needing time to find a place to be woven into the schematic of sonance.

Classical Music is a whole which will last and be handed down to future generations. There may be additional modes, but it will still be a complete genre, incorporating many things in one broad assembly. The circle will be ever widened, but every new part will be a curve which will form a new section of the whole rather than being an independent world of its own.

7.   Transport

Music is art without walls. When you enter it, you are outside wherever you have been before. Music transports you. There is a sort of "You Are There" immediacy to it that is missing from most other art forms with the exception of motion pictures.

Probably one of the greatest horrors in life would be confinement. It doesn't have to be being shut up in a prison cell or in a hospital room. It can be being stuck in a job, a situation that is depressing, a relationship that is wearing. All these things call for escape. Some may not be escapable physically or morally, but even if we cannot escape from physical circumstances or the consequences of our choices, we can escape in spirit through the realm of music.

I have already touched on the fact that music carries me where I have never been and brings ideas and emotions to me where I am. When I hear music, I can feel in my head and in my entire spirit that I am somewhere or sometime else than where I am. I can go there without leaving the room.

Classical Music transports me to different places, times, events, feelings, emotions, periods, cultures. It doesn't speak through anything else, but speaks to us directly in such a way that we understand it without auxiliary knowledge. It does this in a way that even literature or the visual arts do not. In viewing a film, you may have to know the general cultural background of the situation or you will feel like you've just fallen down a rabbit hole. The first time I saw "Crouching Tiger Hidden Dragon" I felt that there was a whole unspoken back story which would have enabled me to make more immediate sense out of what I was seeing if they had just added a little narration to that effect at the beginning of the film. I had to read between the lines and scenes to piece it out.

Music can carry anyone without requiring prior informational understanding. Music has this capability because it goes straight to the heart. I do not need an interpreter or subtitles. Music is a direct connection to composers and performers and their varied worlds. The heart can process it.

The arts carry me around the world. D'Indy's "Symphony on a French Mountain Air" takes me to the mountains. Arnold Bax's "November Woods" takes me for a fall nature walk, regardless of the time of year or of the place in which I am living. I first heard both those pieces when I lived in Los Angeles. I didn't need to take a plane to Britain or France. I was there. Many times, now, I play Bax's tone poem in the month of November, and it especially seems to add to my Thanksgiving time.

Incorporating the animal sounds brings nature into the music. I have never been in the arctic, but Rautavaara's "Cantus Arcticus" has taken me there on the ice. I've always felt it was a sort of cousin of that other great nature sound work, "And God Created Great Whales" by Alan Hovhaness which takes me under the surface of the ice and the ocean. Hovhaness is almost single handedly "the" composer of transport. Everything I hear by him takes me somewhere.

Music from the past evokes other times. Chant takes me to the middle ages. It's not just old music, but music infused with an era. I appreciate the dedication and work of the monks, particularly in their copying and transmission of the New Testament. Their music not only takes me to that time of monastic seclusion, but it brings me back.

I will never be able to get into a time machine and go to the Esterhazy court, but every time I hear the "Farewell Symphony", I can almost see the faces of those in the audience, wondering what was up. One recording I heard many years ago on the radio had each departing musician say auf Wiedersehen as he or she played their last note in the piece. It may have originally been a protest method of bringing the plight of the musicians to their patron, but it has become an everlasting connection from me back to the composer who was so clever in speaking without words.

Music is event connected. Sousa always goes with patriotic proceedings in America. The Blue Danube signals the end of the Vienna New Year's Day concert. Pomp and Circumstance brings the Proms concerts right up to the end in its home country and processes graduates down the aisle around the world. Music tells us what is happening in our lives.

Music can also connect us to past events. I was so moved in my early days of Classical Music experience in the Mercury Living Presence album containing Tchaikovsky's "1812 Overture" on one side and Beethoven's "Wellington's Victory" on the other. I experienced time travel when I heard this music. I also experience it in the recording of Beethoven's 9th put on at the time of the fall of the Berlin wall and in hearing Tan Dun's "Symphony 1997" which accompanied the handover of Hong Kong from Britain back to China. I wasn't at either of those events, but I can feel what it was like to be there from listening to the recordings.

Music adds to experiences by heightening them. Seasonal music is what makes the seasons for me, even more than the decorations. Distressing times are relieved by peaceful or joyful music as King Saul found out when David played. Music can take a non-event day and make something out of it.

Feelings and emotions seem to be almost the same thing. It could be that feelings are distinguished as being more fleeting, while emotions are more abiding. The feeling is the initial reaction to something. The emotion is its home in your psyche. Music plays us as much as it does itself.

Individual instruments can affect us in particular ways. Organ music has taken a hit in popular culture. It's either pictured as tremendously boring or else as connected with some megalomaniac in the movies playing it to calm his nerves or to rouse himself to some new deviltry. But, it's not either one of those.

Love of the organ is a specialized genre of instrumental likes. We don't hear it as much as we do the piano. There are fewer organs in public venues today, but, when they are played, they are particularly indomitable. They dig deep inside us. When Bach is played we feel the notes. Very few instruments can do that. I couldn't stand up and give a scholarly explanation of a toccata, but when I hear one of Bach's, it does something to me.

At the other end, our emotions can be roused by a brass ensemble to fever pitch or calmed down by a flute's gentle whisperings. We are carried to the center of our hearts where something is always being done. It's not that music is a magic which will change every depression to a joy, but it is there to help.

I've cited instruments, but it is not those alone which can accomplish this. The initial notes of Beethoven's Fifth served to unite the nations to victory in World War II. They were played over and over, but until the victory came, no one was tired of them, for they expressed a desire to see the day of peace once again. Because I didn't live in that era, those notes don't speak the same patriotic sentiment to me, but they still express a swelling of the heart, which is probably why they were tied into the victory cry to begin with.

Periods of history are expressed by music. I

can see the wigs and large dresses when I hear a minuet. Gershwin takes me to the jazz era from the opening clarinet solo in "Rhapsody in Blue". By recording, I can go where I want, at will. And, I can come back to where I am without missing a heart beat.

Classical Music is a great culture transmitter. I can appreciate something about someone else when I hear their music. I can hear Chinese music, and it says something. It is never incomprehensible to me as Chinese characters on a page are.

Music is the only way we can be in two places at one time. I go somewhere when I listen. Even if the music is in the remote background, I'm still somewhere more than where I would be were there no music about at all. Not everyone loves to travel, but I do, and music can take me more places than I could ever go in a lifetime.

And one more thing about the transporting element of music. Maybe you haven't experienced this, but I often do. This kind of music is almost always over before I'm ready to be done. Listening on a recorded medium, I can play it over again, but I really noticed it in the concert hall recently. I was listening to George Crumb's "Vox Balaenae". When the piece was done, it was done, and they took their music and instruments (except for the piano) and went off stage to go on with their lives. I wasn't ready for that, but I guess I had to go on with my life, too. Music which transports can so consume the person that time almost disappears.

8.   Threshold

Music is evidence of something beyond ourselves. It invites us to go where we have not gone before.

I don't know if I can do an adequate job in describing this next concept, but at least I can give you a peek at it. Transport is the phenomenon of the music taking you somewhere. Threshold is the phenomenon of opening the door for you to go somewhere by your own action. It won't take you there, but it provides a glimpse of it and often outlines the path to follow to reach it. At the very least it provides direction.

We do not live in a two dimension "Flatland" world, but the universe is more than three dimensional. There is a spiritual realm which cannot be placed on a grid alongside the there dimensions space. It is an additional factor like time. I understand that fact by revelation. Fairy stories speak of the beyond, but even their tellers don't "believe" in them as realities. They are told as "fairy" stories, and not as documentary non-fiction or historical novels of events which could have taken place, but didn't.

Reality doesn't have to be seen to be real. It doesn't have to be handled to be definite. It doesn't have to be tasted to satisfy. Neither does it have to stay "out there". It can enter into our hearts. We can go to it. Direction is not really for the purpose of enlightening our end of things, but for the purpose of showing a destination. There are destinations outward away from us, upward above us, and even inward inside us.

Music is one of the thresholds across which we can go to the beyond. It works better than a looking glass. It doesn't have to slip through a warp or worm hole to enter a parallel universe. Music may be the closest art form to faith, itself. It makes us aware of the unseen.

When we hear the spiritual in music, we are hearing reality. Music leaves a lasting impression. It permanently opens the door to hidden spaces. Even if we do not remember all the notes, we retain the impressions they made on our spirits.

That hint of the beyond was what drew me to Rachmaninov's second symphony. There was a new tug at my spirit the very first time I heard the opening moments of the work. The world around me was commonplace and filled with unending duties such as school and chores. This piece spoke of things outside the realm of what I was then experiencing. It spoke of depths and heights to which I could go.

Sometimes it only takes a moment to make a difference, and music can provide moments tucked away in the middle of a piece. One such moment comes somewhere around the minute or minute and a half mark of the third movement of Bantock's Celtic Symphony. Bantock isn't a major name, but he is much more than an also ran. That moment, when I recently heard it again, created a kind of spike of energy in it. I don't know if it would do that when I hear it again, but it did this time. Music is valuable because we can pick up more from it than the notes themselves. We live in the moments as much as in the stream of time, and it's no wonder that that's where these things will find us. You have to listen or the moment will escape you.

A piece which I first heard on the radio in college which does this is Gustav Holst's "Hymn Of Jesus". I learned many years later, after I'd been listening to the piece for probably close to 40 years, that the text is a Gnostic one, and while I do not believe in the inspiration of the Gnostics, I love the music of this piece. I couldn't really understand all the words, anyway, so I don't feel like I'm going down the wrong path. What I am hearing is things which are beyond this present realm. The music testifies that there is something more there.

More recently, I have noticed that phenomenon in some of the Christmas music I've been listening to such as Lutoslawski's "Twenty Polish Christmas Carols" or William Mathias' "Ave Rex". These are not the familiar carols and holiday tunes. "Silent Night" and "Jingle Bells" can always be counted on to put us in the holiday mood. They say what they say without providing any interior adventures, but these "new to me" classical pieces testify of the realities beyond the music itself.

My mind is always drawn beyond when I hear the Lutoslawski and Mathias. I don't know what the words of the Polish songs means, but I do know that Ave Rex means Hail King. It is not the particular words which speak to me, though. Even if they were all translated into English, what would come through is the dedication to Jesus woven into the music.

Olivier Messiaen is in a class by himself. His music is unlike anyone else's. It took me a while to like him when I heard him on the radio, but long before I had even formulated my thoughts on this concept of the threshold, I knew that in his music I was listening to something beyond. I just recently got a cd set of his music, some of which I had heard, but most of which was new to me. That sense of listening "through the looking glass" is very strong in his music. It's not that the music is quirky or thought provoking, but that it comes out of a realm beyond.

On a more traditional level we have Rodrigo's "In Search Of What Lies Beyond". The first time I heard it on the radio, I didn't know what he was searching for, but I was transported. Since then, I have learned that the piece was commissioned by the Houston symphony as a tribute to that area's part in space exploration. Even though we stay in the universe in this piece, we are getting off our planet. The music doesn't take us there in a documentary linear sort of way such as Villa Lobos' "Little Train of the Caipira" (a piece I first heard as a child and which I still love) does, but it gives testimony that something more is there, and it challenges us to go to it, however we can.

The greatest reality is God Himself. Even people who don't claim there is a God still believe in some ultimate reality. There is no one who operates in a vacuum without something above him. Our greatest composers have testified to the supreme being, although often in different ways. Bach had a sense of God. He wrote of God in the Now. Handel gave us "The Messiah", but his was a sense of God in the Past. I am exalted when I hear Handel, but I am transported when I hear Bach.

Elevator music won't even take you up one floor. You have to push the button for that. At the most, it's designed to keep the cattle quiet and undisturbed on their rides, but real music can act as an elevator to places the Otis company never took anyone to.

Do you want to go somewhere? Do you want to meet a heart unlike any you have ever met? You may not have an actual place or person in mind, but you may want to go where something wonderful would take place or where you would come to a fulfillment never before experienced. It is very possible that music will take you or at least get you to the jumping off point, if you can find the right music.

Not every music works for everyone. It doesn't have to. That's where diversity is a good thing. Some have found the door open through chant, but for others the door is nailed shut by chant. In the end, it's probably a matter of serendipity rather than of pursuit.

The music won't do it all. When you come to the threshold, music's responsibility ends and yours begins. You have to pass over to what is beyond. Music is only a guide. You are the traveler.

Since we are talking about ultimate realities and values, I am convinced that the call to them will be there, whether you find the music for it or not. The music helps to identify or introduce. It may make it easier to go out there. It may provide a better moment of receptivity. Cross the threshold and discover a new world every day. I love music because it opens doors.

9. Forefront Vs Background

Back in the 80s, I once spoke with a lady who was probably just a year or two older than me, who was somewhat of a purist in terms of church music. She felt that the music should never be used for offering or communion "meditations", etc. She felt that it cheapened the music. In effect, she was saying that all music should be in the forefront. I disagree. I feel that both forefront and background uses of music are valid in the church and in the world at large.

That which is in the forefront is there to the exclusion of everything else. Even though I listen to recorded music in the background when I read at home, I would never read a book during a concert hall presentation. There, the personal performance makes an immediate connection. The musicians are in front of me, and so is the music. There is nothing in the world, but the music I am hearing.

When I am at home or in the car, though, it's another matter. I need music as a backdrop for the scenes of my day. Sometimes, I have it on in social settings, but then I catch myself wanting to listen to the piece rather than the person, so I've taken to leaving the music off when we have people over. Interaction doesn't need a background. Most of the time, though, in public, music relaxes the atmosphere and makes it more possible to relate to others. It makes conversations easier because our words don't stick out so much in our own awareness. It's as if we have a cushion around us.

As well as being a declaration of the value of Classical Music, this book is a kind of user's manual, pointing out what happens and making suggestions for allowing more things to happen. We can do something with our music. If we just had to submit to it, it would hardly be pleasurable. It is what we accomplish with it, and what it does for us, that makes us love it.

I remember when Silly Putty was a new product. It was greatly touted on television, and, while we weren't the first on our block to have some, we eventually did get it. You could bounce it, mold it, copy newspaper pictures with it, and I don't know what all else. It was a multi-use toy, and that was its selling point. I think that may well be the reason why it is still in production today when so many of the more "glamorous" toys of my childhood are forgotten. I can remember wanting, but not getting, dinosaurs which shot little darts and signal sets which would enable you to contact the neighbor boy after you were both supposed to be in bed, but I haven't seem them around lately. They died because they were relatively limited in what they offered compared to the versatile Silly Putty.

Classical Music has an even greater versatility. It can be used in so many different ways. Some of them are forefront ways, such as in the concert hall. Others are the background. Some pieces can be used both ways.

I always have some kind of Classical Music on when I read, and especially as I am writing this book. It doesn't matter what mood the music is. For the most part, I work better with it there. Maybe I am afraid of silence, as many city dwellers seem to be, but music is more than the city's cacophony providing a background which may not be comfortable, but which is familiar. It is a unifying point in my thinking and feeling.

Different composers take different places in our experience. A single form, the serenade, for example, can be both background and foreground. Mozart's serenades could be in the background of our live while Dvorak's serenades require more attentive listening. We can use our music in more than one way.

Music can add to, enhance or define your experience. Later we will discuss its power to enhance seasons or events, but, in every day listening we can often do so much more if music is at our side.

In one sense, when I'm listening to music and typing this book, I'm getting away with doing two things at the same time. That gives me a sense of double accomplishment. It also enables me to listen to what I wouldn't have enough time to listen to if I could only listen when I devoted myself exclusively to the listening experience. I have such a large collection, after almost fifty years of collecting, that there is no way I could listen to everything I own even in the space of a single year.

Some things only bounce up from the stacks every several years, but when they do, they are often like a new discovery which then requires listenings of greater frequency. Doing double duty with my time allows me to find those instead of losing them. I believe it also helps me to find thoughts and skills and productivity. Music meshes with my soul for synergy.

Music can be a focus in our background. I once heard an author who absolutely discounted the idea that music and thinking go together. His was a specific reaction to the theory which had been going the rounds that listening to Mozart increases intelligence or whatever that claim was. Maybe, Mozart's music increased nothing in him, but no one can make a blanket statement for others based on their own experience when it comes to music. In the world of psychology, for every series of tests which supports one premise, there is another series of tests which could support an opposite premise. Sometimes, it has nothing to do with the results, but the biases built into the testing procedure to begin with.

I will ignore the test results of others on this matter, and go by my own. Classical Music starts my thinking processes going, and things come out that wouldn't come out any other way. If music stunts your thinking, then, by all means, turn it off when you are thinking, but don't make a rule about it for anyone else, and don't let anyone make a rule for you until you know the effect of the music on your thinking. Only you know what you need and can use in your background.

In the forefront, music focuses us together with others. This is why concerts are so rousing. Every time I hear a recording of one of the New Year's Day concerts from Vienna, I want to clap along on the Radetzky March. That's a piece that you have to stop what you are doing and get in on, even if you've got the Strauss cd on in the background. If you're driving and have to clap, then just pull over and do it. It's not that long a piece, and you'll be safe.

In the background, music melds us together with others. Music is never just about ourselves, but about our relationship to our God, our family, our community, our nation, our world. As I said, music is in heaven. Along with love, it's about the only thing we experience here which will be experienced there, only I believe we'll have to put it in the forefront category, but then maybe not. Someone Else will be in the forefront. Music can help us even appreciate our God.

10. Shield And Plumb Line

We love music for itself; we love it because it does things for us, even more than what we've spoken of so far. It opens doors to and in us. It takes us places and unites us with others. Before getting real specific about myself, I would like to look at two more functions of music, one with regard to external things, and the other with regard to our deepest interior.

Music can be in front of you or beside you. You can get inside it. Other works of art stay exterior to you, but you can get inside music. This is because it happens while you are experiencing it. A painting or sculpture is there, but you have to bring your appreciation or understanding to it, in order for it to function inside you. It ceased to "happen" once the artist laid down his tools. A piece of literature becomes something to you because you break it down off the page through the process of reading it. But, music happens around you. It happens whether you are there or not. It is never imprisoned inside its materials, but is always alive in performance. This has a great value, not simply on the experiential level, but on the practical level as well.

Sometimes, music can act as a shield, protecting us from outside stress and allowing us to move freely in a realm where we might be overwhelmed. My wife, Jeanette, and I always notice the difference when we are in a restaurant with no music. We seem to stick out. Our presence is more public than we would like it to be. Light music in the background keeps the conversations of others away from our ears and ours away from theirs, hopefully. I don't know whether it gives us something positive to concentrate on instead of what they are saying or if it masks their voices so that they become part of an indistinguishable background curtain of sound. It could be that the music is what we make sense of consciously, and we let the words of others, which we have no right to hear anyway, pass into oblivion. Whatever happens, it works to give us some space in public.

Music insulates from the world around us in other ways. It creates a safe space, one which is familiar to us and which can keep at bay for a time the forces of others to enter our consciousness. We are never prepared for the siren out of the blue, but that doesn't weigh us down as much as the constant invasion of others does. There is a time for reaching out to the people around us, but there is also a time for a quiet rest inside our own space.

Back to the restaurant setting, for example, we don't really want to know all about the troubles or triumphs of other diners. We were once having a dinner at a nice restaurant in Solvang, California. This was over thirty years ago. We never did know the names of the ladies at the table next to ours, but we certainly knew of their Christmas gift giving "woes". One lady complained to the other that she was only able to give $5,000.00 worth of gifts to one person on her list that year. We have joked about that for years, but we didn't really want to know it, and our dining experience would have been so much pleasanter if we hadn't had to cope with this "difficulty" which we have never had to face ourselves. Of course, they could have controlled their tongues and spoke in softer tones or waited until they were in private to speak of such things, but a little music might have helped there.

Music creates a world of its own and so it gives privacy. I noticed this when I used to travel on the blue line in the Los Angeles area years ago. There were more people on a single train than I normally see in a single week in my rural existence now. Listening on headphones helped keep perspective. It was like a curtain I could retreat behind. I've also used it in a public men's group journaling setting where it helps me to set aside conversations and disturbing radio commentaries around me so as to focus on what I am studying during the time where each man is writing down his own thoughts.

In the middle of the fast and furious, music allows us to heal and catch our breath. The beat regulates thinking and can get us out of the circle of the rat race. It can help us slow down or sometimes speed us up, if necessary. The military has recognized this musical value for years in the marches which so move everyone who hears them. We recently heard a wind orchestra playing "Stars

And Stripes Forever". Because it was done in a concert setting, I found it to be a bit wimpy, but when I heard the Paris City Band play it on the 4th of July, I was ready to get up and march. Such music shields us from complacency.

Other things can be a shield, but there is nothing which also can build us up at the same time. Music plumbs our depths. Like a plumb line, it shows the contours of our interior and registers the profundity of our thinking and feeling about various things.

Music works from the inside out. Sometimes we discover our feelings about things when we hear music.

Later on I'll be discussing Sousa and this phenomenon, but a little of it belongs here. I had heard his music all my life and was "used to" it and took it for granted (the worst thing that can happen to music, even more terrible than detesting it), but one day I turned a corner and saw the truth of all the things his music was saying, and it was all new again. I saw that those things were things I believed in – order, growth, movement, involvement, the United States of America. It is a fierce love, not simply of our country, but of the eternal ideals our country is built upon which is embodied in his music.

There are other discoveries to be made, and music can help find them. This is not a case of music creating thinking in us, but of exposing or bringing to the surface the viewpoints which we already have.   We discover the depths of our feelings about things when we hear music about those things.   When we know how deep a thing runs in us, we know how truly important it is.   We not only plumb the depths, but show what runs straight through us as a plumb line does.

Music can help us in assessing our own hearts and our own world.   Music works on both our outside and inside.   That is one reason it is such an effective art form.   The shield keeps the pernicious at bay.   The plumb line helps us to straighten up.   It helps us to build from what we hear.

We discover the important and keep it important.   It is something we can communicate to others.   It gives motivation for good deeds or attitudes.   It is good in a world of evil.

11.   Music Talks

There is no end to what music does for us. How it does it is often unknown, even to us who experience it, but its effects are real. It can be work good apart from our awareness.

Recently, as I was listening to a recording of Beethoven's cello sonatas, it came to me that not only does the music speak to me, but, in this particular case, it could speak for me.

I wasn't in any kind of mood that day, but all of a sudden I recognized that what was being said was true of me. It's not that there was some specific message that I could put into words, but it seemed to be speaking me. I don't know that that is a grammatical phrase, to some that music speaks me, but it expresses what I'd like to. Besides being persons, we are also something of a language, a medium for communication. If we are silent, we are lessened. If we are spoken, we can be known.

The cello has the right range for melancholy soul searching sort of music to begin with, and I am, on the scale of the four Greek temperaments, definitely an introverted melancholy. Beethoven was speaking of deep things in the heart, the kinds of things which rarely make it out into the open just because they are deep. For one moment as these pieces are being played or listened to they are not buried, but out in the open. To have someone speak us is very unusual and valuable.

We all have things that we don't know how to

put into words. Sometimes, we are afraid to speak for fear of the consequences or lack of consequences, but music has no fear. There is no guarantee that others will hear what the music is saying for us, but we know that we are being expressed in a concrete manner whether anyone understands it or not. We know that we are articulated in the universe.

Music is a universal language. I never learned but a few words of German, yet I understand Bach and Beethoven and Haydn, German speakers all, I believe, perfectly. I know no Italian other than the few terms that have crept their way into broad usage or which are used in musical notations, yet I never am in doubt about Vivaldi or Verdi, even in their choral works which are sung in Italian. Music speaks of emotions and thoughts. It speaks of the inner person and their contact with the outer world. Folk music from obscure tribes around the world, while it is totally out of the stream of my schematic, says something which conveys more than gestures or body language would.

Music articulates. Even modern pieces such as the one by John Cage using cacti as instruments says something. We may not regard Cage's cacti or crumpled paper as instruments. We may not resonate with Ligeti's 100 metronomes, either, but they are articulate. We may not like the pieces themselves or the whole concept of objects creating music, but they speak. There are times when all we can speak is in screams and cries, so maybe there is some validity for these things which do the same.

We live in a world which was begun by the words of God, "Let there be..." The universe is not expected merely to exist. The Psalms speak in figurative words of various parts of creation communicating. We talk of music of the spheres. It's there in the universe. Creation continues to speak and sing.

It's as if my inner mood is out in the open where it can be examined and encountered by others and dispelled or heightened, whichever is necessary. I am affirmed.

Even depressing music has its place. It can transfer the mood to the music and exorcise it from the heart. I don't know if David's music played before Saul was happy or sad, as we conceive of it, but whatever it was, Saul was the better for it. Of course, there was a spiritual force behind it as a cause of calming Saul as well as the music.

No one can change apart from understanding. Melancholy music can remove melancholy, just as happy music can bring in joy. We understand well the infectiousness of a snappy tune. We're livened up by a Strauss waltz or a Sousa march. Those are basics, and sometimes they are forgotten because they are so basic and we have taken them for granted, but they do fulfill their functions.

On the other hand, by experiencing misery or despair in music, we feel that we are able to speak and understand ourselves. This says what we are and what we are feeling, and once that is understood, we can change.

When the music speaks **for** me, I can relax for I know I am known. I can even be more objective about myself.

Someone else has to have known their own heart in order to have created such music. I am in fellowship. We are not alone.

12. Experience And Memory

I keep seeing other aspects of this. That in itself marks this as valuable. Like all culture it is more than a commodity or a mark of erudition. It is a thing in which we live.

Some of this has been discussed in bits and pieces already, but I'd like to put them all together here as a whole.

Music goes beyond itself. What you hear is not all there is. It is not simply notes and timing. If that were the case we could program perfection into a computer and get an exact note and timing, but there would be no soul to it. Perfection is not what we need; it's connection.

Music gives me an experience. Because I love this music I am guaranteed an experience whether I go to the concert hall (which is not dead as Glenn Gould supposed it to be) or listen to a recording. It's not something that passes the time, but time through which I pass. Of course, we experience time whether we want to or not, but so many times we wish we could control it. We would like to hurry it up when it is too slow or slow it down when it rips through us. Music, at least when you are choosing a recording to listen to, is the type of time that you can control by your selection of what you hear or play. It gives a shape to time that the clock never gives.

I like experiences. I think most people do. That's why we travel. We could read about a place or a sensation, but that would never take the place of being there. All the finest poetry or prose in the world about a bowl of ice cream cannot even come close to the experience of dipping your spoon in it and putting it full in your mouth and savoring the entire flavor and texture of the ice cream. Music is almost like ice cream for the ears, only it's not fattening.

As I listen to a piece, I am passing through it. A book or movie can create an experience, but not like music does. Those spell everything out, but music is something of an adventure which I come to on the spot every time I hear it. I can hear the same piece more than once and have a different experience each time.

I have a suspicion that people who don't like music don't make any attempt at all to experience it, and, of course, then they don't. They just "get through it". I know I did enough of that with some of the pieces I played when I was first learning the piano, but the older I get the more I find that things are not exhausted that easily. At times if I'm playing the piano I tend to go on and on until I'm forced to a stopping place because of schedule. I can do that with recorded music as well. I have gone back and heard something over a time or two more before going on to another piece. It can be a building experience in which my inside is stretched out and filled all at the same time.

When I listen to music it creates other things inside me. Sometimes it's a picture. Sometimes it's a feeling. I'm never quite sure whether those things were there before and the music just brought them out into the open or whether they were thoughts I never would have had apart from the music.

My interior landscape is always shifting and changing. As a child I was fascinated by the kaleidoscope with its ever changing shapes and colors, all created out of a few bits of plastic or whatever it was that was inside them then. The images I saw there didn't "mean" anything, but they always gave delight. That may be one of the premier marks of good experience that it gives delight. You don't have to explain it or expound it, only let it wend its way through your consciousness.

In the end, music leaves me with a memory. It doesn't vanish without a trace. Only something which has been experienced can do that. It's not always a memory of the notes or timing or tunes, but of the feelings and impressions I had. It can be simply a memory of having felt better than I felt before.

Memory can be a guide to going back to re-experience the music or it can be an impetus to do what the experience stirred up inside you.

I've spoken of some pieces that transported me or were threshold pieces. Those are examples of what I'm talking about.

As I'm writing this it's the Christmas season. As you'll see in the listing on seasonal music below, I have a lot to listen to. One piece I hear every year which I haven't heard yet is Vaughan Williams'

"Hodie". It's about 50 minutes of beautiful modern choral music climaxing in a movement with words by Milton. I will be listening to it again. It is more than a record of the birth of Jesus. It is an expression of the power and wonder and cosmic significance of it all. I experience the wonder and then I remember Jesus. Music often reminds of the reality that it has only intimated, and it's not jealous when we go there. It wants to lead us and take us. It gives us something to draw on when we can't hear it.

As you listen or play, experience it and then remember it. You may not go back to it. You may be led to go somewhere else, but you will go because music is like that. It stirs us to better things.

13. Likes And Dislikes

Like everyone else, I have my likes and dislikes. Boiled down and put in a single framework, they form my schematic. I will be speaking in general terms in this chapter. The next chapter will give some particulars in depth.

What is in my schematic is music which is a part of me. I'm at home with it. I feel comfortable with it. It is not just familiar, but deliberately familiar. I have chosen to be accustomed to it. I know what it is, and I'm holding on to it. Even if a person doesn't seem to be conscious of an internal schematic, it always goes into action when he is met by something new or unfamiliar. It weighs what is new against what is known and valued. Then it is judged by whether or not it fits into the schematic.

This whole schematic matter works in general culture as well, and also with non-Classical Music. After all, something which works in one realm should work in another as well if it is a valid truth.

After reading Sloboda's article (cited in the introduction), I came to see that he had explained the problem which had been plaguing church music, too, for the preceding decades. Up until the 1970s, church music was pretty much a unified field. You could go into almost any church in America, thumb through their hymn book, and find probably 90% or more of the songs in them to be ones you knew. Then, with the advent of the overhead and computer projection system, everything changed.

No longer were the churches bound by what was in the hymn books which were too expensive to change out for an entire congregation more than every twenty or thirty years. The "Praise and Worship" songs rose up. They were a vastly different kind of music than the established hymns. They weren't just a horse of a different color. They weren't even a horse. (I guess you can tell which side I'm on.)

We won't really know in our life time whether "Praise and Worship" songs are here to stay or not, because that kind of music requires centuries to be permanently retained, but what we have had is a clash between the old camp holding to the hymns and the new camp holding to the choruses. It is a clash of schematics.

In the classical world, the schematics clashed most resoundingly in the 1913 premiere of "The Rite Of Spring". Very seldom is there such an overt passing from one era to another as there was with this peace. I made sure to listen to in a recording conducted by Stravinsky himself on 29 May 2013, the hundredth anniversary of the premiere. My theory is that it wasn't that people didn't like dissonance, but that it was not a part of their schematic, and they didn't know what to do with it. Usually, when people don't know what to do with something, they end up rejecting it. What we reject often becomes the grounds for the condemnation of those who accept it.

What I listen to says something about who I

am. It doesn't say everything, but it does say something. It doesn't say something about or against anyone else. Everyone has a right to his own schematic. Your liking something I don't like doesn't impinge on my schematic. It is totally outside it, but too many people want to make their taste be your guide.

I don't assign moral values to notes and their intervals as I heard a Christian speaker once do. He was citing some other so-called "authority" on the issue, and I don't have the original material available to cite that author, so I cannot comment other than to say that there is nothing moral or immoral about notes or intervals or rhythms, themselves. Rejection of anything with regard to these things is simply an assertion of schematic, not a genuine moral judgment.

There is a connection between the arts and the personality. What we create and what we appreciate are a part of the creating of the circle we spoke of earlier. What we need in life is not so much good music, as good character. For me, unless music espouses the cause of sin, and that espousal almost certainly requires words, it is open to appreciation. I often appreciate works about matters I would not agree with theologically or philosophically. I am not a socialist, and yet I enjoy the music of Shostakovich and Prokofiev created in and regimented by a rigid social regime. By listening to music created in a communist state, I am not endorsing communist ideology. I listen because the music stands on its own apart from the prevailing politics of the day. To me, Shostakovich's music doesn't say ideology; it say heart, and that's how we should receive it.

What do I prefer? Here is a list of my musical inclinations in broad general terms. Some of this will be fleshed out in a following chapter. It is not absolute, as some specific pieces in the lower ranked forms may be more enjoyed than some specific pieces in the higher, which would be the veridical at work, but this is an outline of my schematic:

1.   Symphonies and Straight Orchestral music such as tone poems and ballets.

These have almost always been at the top of my list. I don't know whether this is because of my early exposure to those pieces which first drew me to the music or whether I just prefer them. I like just about any symphony, from the early ones of Haydn to those of ultra modern composers such as Carter and Rautavaara.

2.   Concertos, in the following order of preference - piano, violin, guitar, flute, then other instruments.

The flute is there because of Jean Pierre Rampal. The piano, being my own instrument, although I could not begin to play any classical concerto,   is   the   most   versatile antagonist/conspirator to the orchestra, probably, for the most part, because it is not a part of it as the violin or flute are. The two elements set one another apart and astound in their cooperation.

3.   Chamber music with the string quartet on the top.

I appreciate the trios of Beethoven and Dvorak and the quintets and other number groupings, but the quartet is the absolute basic. The quintet, to take one of the closest relatives of the quartet, is a little fuller and looser. It probably involves some doubling of notes by the players, but in the quartet, everyone has his own note which is not duplicated by any other. The quartet is tighter and more personal than any other chamber ensemble. It is the perfect number of voices to carry a full conversation. The dialogue is clearer between the instruments. It's balanced better than a trio. The quartet is just the right number of voices in the string arena; on the other hand, the quintet format works for brass, as we see in the Canadian Brass and all similar ensembles. In the earlier string quartets, such as those of Haydn, we see harmonization at work. This shows cooperation. In the later string quartets, such as those of Carter, which I am listening to as I write this, we hear confrontations and disagreements, but there is resolution. Even if the discussion is resolved in a dissonance, it is resolved, for the four members do not separate themselves from one another to become soloists; they remain a unit all the way.

4.   Instrumental music.

The piano is at the top, followed by Rampal's flute, the guitar, and the organ. I normally like the more balanced work of an ensemble, but the soloist gives us total personality. That may be one reason why I like Glenn Gould so much. I don't know that he's technically superior to Rubinstein, Horowitz, Brendel or Lang Lang, but his personality comes to me through the discs in a way the others' do not. He plays in such a way that you can't just take him or leave him. There is something about him that I like. Maybe it's the fact that he would sing along with himself as he played. You can hear it especially on the last recording of the Goldbergs. He was totally participating in what he was doing. The fact that his voice lay over the piano notes didn't diminish my enjoyment of them. It only made the whole more compelling.

5.   Choral music.

This is the category of the passions, cantatas, masses and oratorios. Because they have more group singing than solos, they are more like a verbal symphony than an opera. Of course, there are symphonies such as Beethoven's 9th and Brian's "Gothic", which employ choirs to great effect by melding them into the symphony as a whole, but they belong in the symphonic category. In addition to the large scale groups, there are those such as Chanticleer and Anonymous 4 who have almost given a new definition to the word "beauty" in terms of music.

As stated earlier, sometimes there is variation in the ordering based on particular pieces. To give one example, Schubert's "Trout" quintet rates much higher with me than any of his symphonies, and my favorite piece of all comes from the fifth category rather than the first.

I have antipathies as well. I mention them, but I make no judgment on anyone who likes what I don't. They are good things. In many ways, the things I don't like are among what may be considered the most exquisite creations of music, but, despite the fact I have tried hard to "like" some of them, they do not have a home in my schematic.

1.   Lieder and songs.

These are my least favorite kinds of Classical Music. I love Schubert's chamber works, symphonies and sacred choral works. I have a seven cd set of the latter which I have listened to many times. But, the lieder, which he seems to have done better than anyone else, do absolutely nothing at all for me, no matter how many times I've tried to pick them up. I always will bypass an album composed exclusively of songs or lieder. The few that I do have are either isolated songs included on discs covering a large range of works or some which have come from the BBC Music Magazine. Lieder is a specially acquired taste.

2.   Opera.

This is a specialized area of Classical Music, almost a sub-genre operating on an entirely different basis than the rest of Classical Music. Many people like Classical Music, but not opera. It seems, although I have no way of verifying it, that people who like opera mostly like only opera. It seems to be a singularity in the Classical Music world. It could that because my focus is only listening, opera doesn't do it for me; it could be that opera must be seen in person to be really appreciated. I like music that blends in with my whole life. Opera needs to be seen as well as heard. I have seen several operas including The Marriage of Figaro, The Flying Dutchman, Il Trovatore, and Paggliaci, but for the most part the music by itself demands more than I'm willing to participate in via recording. One veridical exception is the Wagner Ring cycle. I recently found a set which was so cheap it was almost free, so I decided to give them a whirl since 2013 is the 200th birthday anniversary celebration of Wagner. Actually, I found them very compatible with my schematic, especially as I could imagine that they were choral symphonies.

3.   Pieces with spoken words interwoven into the music.

I like to keep my speaking and my music separate. One of the few exceptions is Martinu's "Gilgamesh". It doesn't have too many words, and many of them are not in English, so I'm not distracted by them. Other veridical exceptions are Stravinsky's "The Flood", the multi-composer "Genesis Suite" and Copland's "Lincoln Portrait". These speak to my faith and patriotism, and I enjoy them, but I never put them on to have in the background. I have to have them in the forefront, always.

There are a few swing votes which could go either way. Some ultra modern works or particular dissonances take a while to get inside my schematic, but they often do if I give them enough listens. Penderecki's "Utrenja" was one of those. A few others never made it in. There was an album I owned once consisting of pieces in which the composer used extreme dynamics. In order to hear the soft parts at all, you blasted yourself out when the loud parts came along. I think I would have liked it if the two ends of the dynamic spectrum had not been so excessive, but I just couldn't enjoy it as it was, and probably wouldn't have enjoyed it in a concert hall. That is the only classical cd I ever bought that went to the Goodwill bin. I didn't wish to betray anyone else by giving it to them.

Music is a real thing that can be examined and liked for what it is. It is not just the absence of silence. More has probably been written about John

Cage's "4'33"" than any other piece he "wrote". I won't say that I "love" his music, but I certainly find it interesting as something way on the outskirts of the classical music universe perimeter. However, I'm on the side of those who are not so sure that this particular piece can be classified as "music". I once heard a broadcast of a "performance" of it over the internet from the BBC Proms. I cranked up the speakers as loud as I could. I didn't hear music; I only heard audience noises. This is how I put my observations as opinion #327 of chapter 7 in my <u>Book Of Opinions And Observations</u>:

327.   4'33" is a case where, regardless of John Cage's stated intentions in "creating" this piece, because it is without content, everyone who "listens" to it can create his own content; thus, to call it a piece of non-music or anti-music is just as valid as to call it a protest against noise, which, I believe, was Cage's intention.

This piece may force us to focus on the sound panorama around us, but it is not music, for that is definite and concrete, employing notes and timing. Without those elements, "4:33" is not even abstract art for it is not taken out of anything. It might have been called an un-happening in 60s parlance. I would call it non-crete. There has to be something there for me to like or dislike. If anything, the only product of "4:33" is to make me wish I had heard four minutes and thirty-three seconds of something I really liked.

Music communicates something. To me, "4:33" has nothing to say. If the composer isn't going to say anything, and I'm going to have to make it say something, then I say, "Let's hear some

Bach!"

14. Expanding Your Schematic

Before giving a specific, if limited, tour through the world of my schematic, I want to give some advice about the general management of schematics. Mine is my own, and I don't intend that anyone should be my musical clone. Your schematic is always yours, no matter how much of it may overlap with anyone else's. Here, I only offer some principles for being systematic about your own likes.

In looking over this material about expanding the schematic, I realized that I had not given any rationale for consciously having a schematic. Before giving the how, we have to have the why.

The function of a schematic is receiving. The music does not just fly over our heads or off into the blue, but we can internalize it. The schematic helps us to catch what others have thrown because we have a place to put it. It allows us not to drop our connection or to lose it or to have it dissipated into nothingness. Music does not exist for itself; it exists for us.

A larger schematic allows you to connect with more people and ideas. No one can contain all schematics. Only God can do that. But, we can profit by the schematics of others.

Ideas reach us through the acceptable, and that which is a part of our schematic is what has proven to be acceptable to us. An idea can reach us through any musical genre, but we can assimilate it easier if it speaks to us in a musical language we approve of.

Still, it's not all about what we approve of. It is valuable to be able to receive what others have to say, even if we don't always agree with it, simply because in this way we are expressing our value of them.

Love me, love my music may not be the correct way of putting it, but it would certainly appear that hate my music, hate me is the thought that runs through many minds. There is a value in at least being able to listen to what someone else is listening to. We may find it is the key to the heart.

Musical tastes are not automatic. They are often acquired, and sometimes acquired deliberately. Often, the very thing you can't stand at one point becomes the thing in which you come to take refuge. Learning it can mean liking it. In the learning, you grow.

Ownership makes the difference in my relationship to the music. I have noticed that I always listen to an album which is my own over one which belongs to a family member in our home which I could listen to at any time, but which I don't seem to get around to.

One reason people don't love music is that they don't have or know their own schematic. Like Charlie the tuna, they try to be of good taste, according to someone else's definition. You don't have to operate in anyone else's schematic. Develop your own. Start with the things that you like and find other things similar or which move you in the same way. The suggestions in this chapter are just that. They are not imperatives. If you control your own schematic, you will be able to love better.

The great thing about music in our day is that we can repeatedly experience it. Centuries ago, you had to be able to go to where the music was being performed. Even wealthy people might never have heard a particular piece more than once in their lifetime. With the advent of recorded music, I can repeat an experience as often as I like. I'm sure I have heard each of the symphonies of Haydn more times than Esterhazy ever heard them all.

Most of my listening has been done by recorded or broadcast media. Without intending to do so, I became the kind of music consumer Glenn Gould left the concert stage to serve, although I don't agree with his contention that the concert hall is dead. My infrequent attendance has mostly been due to financial reasons and logistics, but also because I think I feel I have more value for my money in something I can re-experience rather than in something I can hear once and never hear again. I think this desire for repeatability has shaped much, if not most, of my schematic.

Even though I have a schematic, I do not regard it as fixed and final. I hope it is not the sin of greed, thought, but the good principle of expanding my horizons, which drives my collection expansion. Many years ago, before I had cd technology, I once looked at my collection of 400 odd classical lps and thought to myself that I had just about everything I could ever have that would fit what I wanted to have (I didn't know the term "schematic" then). I had the basic works of the standard composers. Then, a single label changed my thinking.

Naxos was a real budget label for its time. It's still cheaper than the other labels, but the differential in price between it and the others is now much narrower than it was at the beginning. A generation earlier, there had been the Nonesuch label and its releases of European disks to the American market in an ultra budget line. I have replaced the lps I had from them with other versions on cd, but I have found myself wishing that they would produce a set of those recordings such as Mercury did with it's Living Presence Collections of 2012 and 2013. Other labels, such as RCA and Angel, had their budget lines, but it wasn't until Naxos that things really expanded. This was not just because of the price, but because of the breadth of their catalogue.

Naxos covered the standard repertoire and then introduced composers I had never heard of – William Henry Fry, Geirr Tveitt, Havergal Brian, Nikolay Myaskovsky and many others who I grew to love after an initial sampling of their music. Because the label was so inexpensive, I could, in the early days, get three cds for the cost of one on a more expensive label. This encouraged me to try things I would not have bought had the price been steeper. There were also many composers I had heard of, such as William Grant Still, Glazunov and MacDowell, whose music was now released in a complete, affordable format.

Naxos offered more than anyone ever had within the reach of my finances. The end result for me was a breathtaking expansion of my schematic. Once I started down the road with them, I was able to do it with other record clubs and labels. Bargain bins at record stores and department stores used to offer classical recordings. I hardly see bargain bins of any kinds, let alone classical recordings among them, anymore. Stores where you can go in and hold the music in your hand and look at it before you buy it are becoming scarce. I do 100% of my new music buying on line now, but I can still sometimes make discoveries at garage sales and library sales. Don't look down on a used album. It might be a title no longer commercially available, or it might open up a new direction for you.

I want to enlarge my schematic, at least in terms of pieces and composers, even if not always in terms of styles or genres, but many people are content where they are. I can ultimately only tell you what I have experienced for my own benefit. You can introduce people to music, but you can never force them to like it. In forcing you often create antipathy rather than sympathy.

I've seen kids go to concerts because they "had to", for course credit or because a parent or music teacher made them. I have often wondered about the wisdom of exposing young students to something they don't have a big enough frame of reference to understand and then expecting them to assimilate it. Such things are often, then, associated with forcing rather than free enjoyment.

While it may be necessary for a rounded music education to attend concerts or as a way to expose young people to something new, it's best to let people find their own level in the arts after the possibilities have been pointed out. When you take young people to concerts, let them decide whether they like it or not. Nobody likes to have someone order off the menu for them in life; they like to do that themselves. You can give them a taste of your prime rib, but let them order their hamburger for now. They may not appreciate what you're having, today, but they may remember and order it for themselves the next time.

To expand your schematic you have to try new things. Even if you cannot afford to buy new music, there is much available for free listening online or in on the radio. That's all pot luck, but it's how I first found many of the pieces I now highly value. While it may seem like buying a pig in a poke, you can pick things up at yard sales. Anything you hear may open up a whole new field of thought or interest to you.

After you tasted something new, if it doesn't immediately engage you, give it another listen, later on. Free yourself from your first impression before you hear it again.

When I buy a new recording, I listen to it twice before it is filed on the shelves in my collection. On my first listen, I get a feel for the piece or particular performance. The next listen is to take it in. As a normal course, I usually allow a minimum of a week to elapse before the second time, so that I can come to it fresh and not consumed by my first reaction.

At times, I have an immediate liking to a new work. Some things that didn't grab me the first go round really take off on a second listening. Then, there are those albums which don't "click" on either the first or second listen, but which perk up much later in isolated listenings. This happens many times when I've acquired a set or a large number of albums all at once. I can't take them all in by the initial listenings alone.

It takes a while to make room for some music in my heart. Other times, repeated listening is what expands my schematic as I acquire a sense of understanding of the piece or as it finds a place to attach itself in my emotional framework. Sometimes, though, a recording never does arouse me. There are probably others who are spoken to, though, so its value is not dependent on my non-appreciation.

Let each piece you hear speak to you for itself. Don't listen to your own expectations or the criticisms of others. Sometimes I have preconceived notions about a piece based on either the title or album blurb or previous experience with the same composer or performer. You can't expect any piece or performance to be "more of the same". Many of them are "something else", and it's "something else" that makes life.

How can you find out about more? I offer methods/venues.

1.   The BBC Music Magazine is the only Classical Music magazine I have ever read, but it is so excellent that I don't feel I need another one. There are others out there, but from the promotional materials I have received on them, I never saw a reason to switch. Then, too, there's the free cd that comes as a part of the BBC subscription. Even if the recording of a particular month is not of a style I like, such as lieder, I will hold on to it because it came from them. All their recordings are uniformly excellent. They offer reviews and ads of current albums. They have articles on composers and styles and offer continuing educational features on musical terms. Some of the articles describe what are the best and worst recordings of core repertoire works and then go on to describe what else you could listen to, if you like that particular piece. I recommend this as a primary resource for discovering new Classical Music worlds.

2.   Classical radio or online streaming allows you to hear music without buying it. Our area doesn't have a classical radio station, but I have learned much by listening on the BBC and other websites. I

especially recommend the Proms which are broadcast on BBC Radio every summer, but there are other festivals which are broadcast as well. Many stations keep broadcasts available for a week or more, so that, if you missed the program, you can still listen to it. This is a good place to find out about something new risk free.

3.   Many communities host local festivals and concerts such as the Indiana State University Contemporary Music Festival which takes place every fall in Terre Haute, Indiana. Anyone who is within driving distance should attend this festival. A featured visiting composer once commented that there wasn't anything as good as this festival available in New York City. Each year the work of a contemporary composer is featured, although the works of others are performed throughout the three day event as well. One night features college musicians. Another features a guest soloist or ensemble. The third night features an orchestra. The one which has been in residence since I've been going is the Indianapolis Chamber Orchestra. I cannot say too much good about them. The first night I attended one of these concerts I came home and ordered recordings of pieces which had been performed.

4.   Pay attention to the music credits at the end of a movie if there was something musical in there that intrigued you. All films today give separate

listings of the pieces used. These are some of the last things to appear in the credits. Many times, they use things which will change your musical thinking. "The Sting" brought Scott Joplin back to the public consciousness after decades of indifference. "2001" opened the door to much modern music through the use of Ligeti. At the time it came out, I was a high school student and didn't know much about Classical Music past the era of Tchaikovsky. I discovered Howard Hanson from the use of his second symphony at the end of "Alien". That was the first time I ever looked at a credit, and I bought a copy of the symphony as soon as I could find one. That was long before the internet, and it wasn't always easy to find a specific recording at a record store.

5.   Don't despise the familiar. Sousa was a rediscovery for me in the early 2000s. For you it may be Bach, Beethoven, Tchaikovsky or Mozart, all standard repertoirees. All of these have much unexplored territory outside the few "hits" which are often over-played.

6.   If, among your acquaintances, there is someone who really knows music, consult him or her. The personal element can be helpful. People who really love music are delighted to talk about their favorites. Some, of course, will expect that you will adopt their own particular tastes, but you don't have to. Tell them the kinds of things you like

and ask for suggestions.

By deliberately listening in any situation you may discover new delights; usually one thing leads to another. A good schematic, like a good life, is ever expanding.

As a final note, I offer some suggestions of where to start if you're new to this music. It's not a complete survey of Classical music, but it provides access to varying periods of the music spectrum. Too much is left out. I could list 100 pieces and fail to cover the ground, but here are ten listings of works or groups of works which are all readily available. They are offered to give a glimpse into the breadth of the music. All of these open doors to further things.

- ❖ Any album of Gregorian chant or of medieval music performed by Anonymous 4; this will show you the known beginnings of Western music
- ❖ Bach: Goldberg Variations, Well Tempered Clavier, St. Matthew Passion, B minor mass (for the keyboard works I recommend Glenn Gould, but others will do, too)
- ❖ Handel: The Messiah
- ❖ Haydn: Symphony 44 (sometimes called "Trauer")
- ❖ Beethoven: String Quartet Op 59 no 1 (Razumovsky quartet #1)

- ❖ Chopin: Piano Concerto #2
- ❖ Tchaikovsky: 1812 Overture
- ❖ Ives: The Unanswered Question
- ❖ Hovhaness: And God Created Great Whales
- ❖ Steve Reich: Music For 18 Musicians

15. My Schematic (At Least Part Of It)

Although in the earlier chapter I described my schematic as related to genres, it also includes a lot of composers and themes. What I am about to share is not my entire schematic, but only a representative part of it. When you know even a part of what I like, you'll know more about me.

I should say at the beginning that my schematic is mostly composer driven, rather than performer driven. Oh, I have my favorites like Jean Pierre Rampal, who I was once privileged to hear in person in an evening of music the likes of which will be in heaven, and Glenn Gould, who I've only heard via recording, but my collection and listening habits are mostly built around the composers.

I am going to be very specific and cite particular composers and individual works. There are so many I don't have time to record my thoughts on them all. Non-inclusion here doesn't mean dislike, only that these which are mentioned are the cream at the top of the entire great body of music which forms my schematic.

These are my favorites, and there is a great deal of difference between a scale of favoriteness and one of greatness. Many do not appear on this list. Some of the more notable absences are Mozart, Beethoven, Schubert, Brahms, Liszt and Chopin, not to mention earlier important composers such as Monteverdi or most of the contemporary ones. I have many of their works in my collection, but here

I have tried to share comments on the ones that either meant the most to me or with whom my heart has a special relationship. As with an iceberg, what remains under the surface gives stability and depth to what is seen. I could not and would not give up any composer in my schematic, even those not cited below. Together, they build my internal musical landscape.

I have not read a lot about the composers and their lives or studied them formally in a college setting. Most of my education has come from liner notes, cd booklets and radio comments as well from as the BBC Music magazine. There are a few things that linger from the Bernstein broadcasts, too. The only book I think I ever read on a particular composer was The Bach Reader. Then, there was The Gift Of Music by Jane Stuart Smith and Betty Carlson. It is a good book for giving some general background to the great composers as well as something about the spiritual lives, although it does come at those from a fairly severe Calvinist background and sometimes makes judgments I wouldn't make. I am not going to copy anything from any external source, but to rely exclusively on my listening itself and what has been gained from that over the years.

There are distinctions within the stream. I don't like only one genre or composer to the exclusion of all the rest. They all fit the schematic, but occupy different places in it. I don't like all the same, but I rely on the different composers to do different things.

No one knows why they like anything. They just do. Here are analyses of fifteen composers or groupings of composers which all have a firm place in my schematic with a few side trips to explain why some others are not there. My comments are not standards for anyone else, but merely the explanation of my schematic. After Haydn, Bach and Vivaldi, they're not really listed in any order. In sharing about them I will paint a picture of myself as much as I will of them.

1. Haydn is at the top of my heap. He is my favorite. I come back to him over and over again, especially the symphonies and string quartets. Even if no one had said that he was the father of both, I would feel that. They are his strong point more than the piano concerto was. Mozart was master there.

I want to take a moment to explain the relationship of Haydn and Mozart in my schematic. Everyone else seems to put Mozart as the king of the hill. I have a large number of Mozart recordings, including two complete sets by different orchestras of his symphonies, so you could hardly say I despised him or thought him negligible, but while I like Mozart, I love Haydn. It's as simple as that. Mozart certainly has the head, but Haydn has the heart. It could be that the difference lies in the fact that Mozart was so managed for much of his life and Haydn had to scramble a lot according to what I know of his story. I think that can be felt in their music.

Haydn covered a great deal of ground. I first loved the symphonies from the Nonesuch budget releases. I bought my friend, Chuck Keller, a recording of "The Creation" for his birthday one year. Then I borrowed it after he had listened to it, and loved it, even though I didn't understand a word of the German. I heard it complete before I heard "The Messiah" complete. I was inspired by the sweep and grandeur of his music.

In the past few years, it's been the string quartets that have entranced me. I finally collected the last of them this year. The quartets seem even fresher than the symphonies, although without the extent of their range.

Haydn's symphonies had so many names and themes. I was always fascinated by the "Farewell", number 45. The one before it, "Trauer", was the first of his symphonies that I identified with. It wasn't a depressing work, as the German name which means sorrow or grief implied, but one which had a heart deep down to it. I now have recordings of the symphonies by many orchestras and the complete set by Adam Fischer and the Austro-Hungarian Orchestra. They still hit the mark head on.

I never get tired of Haydn. I don't know whether that has more to do with him or with me, but I really think it is his freshness which prevails. Every time I listen, even to a piece I have heard many times, I come away with a sense of his heart. He always looked a little austere in his portraits, but somehow I think he would be able to set a person at their ease. He certainly did with his music.

2.   Bach.
      Let   us   rather   say

BACH.

JOHANN SEBASTIAN BACH!!!

From what I read off a back liner note once, his sons thought him old fashioned, and even some of our contemporaries feel about Bach like Lucy did about Beethoven, saying "What's so great about Bach?" I would pose a different question: What's not great about Bach?

I don't always "like" him in the way I like Haydn or Vivaldi, but it is impossible not to resonate with his music. Order, completeness, connection to God and man -- they are all there. He provides a frame to life and thinking. Bach is almost more an object of veneration than a man to be loved.

I got the Brilliant Classics set of the complete works a few years back, and I'd like to get the Bachakademie one, also, if I ever could quit buying other music long enough to save up for it. Even after getting the Brilliant set, I got rid of very few of the other Bach recordings I had. You can't ever have too much Bach. This is the one composer you **_should_** listen to.

Bach could, and did, do it all – vocal, instrumental, orchestral. There are possibly some individual compositions by others which might excel some of those of Bach, but no one has ever produced a body of work which has stood the test of time as his has. I only wish he could have lived as much as even one year longer and given us that much more.

The Passions and the B Minor Mass stand at the head of the entire procession. I bought a recording of the St. Matthew from a bargain bin when I was in college. It was not done by any of the leading ensembles, but the power in the work was overwhelming from the first time I heard the opening notes. Now, I can pop three cds in my changer (I have two versions) and let it go, but then I had to turn over the 8 sides of the 4 disks to hear the whole work. It's no wonder that in the history of music, one of the great dates is 11 March 1829 when Mendelssohn reintroduced the world to this MASTERWORK.

The greatest recording of the B Minor I have is that done by the Robert Shaw Chorale in 1960. According to the liner notes, they went into the studio with this after spending weeks on the road with it. I can testify from personal experience that performance gets tight, not from practice, but from performance. Any time I was on the road with a group, at the end of that time we were the best we had ever been up to that point, due to the constant refining of singing in public.

Of course, there are hundreds of cantatas and other vocal works. They never seem like so much sausage when I listen to them. I haven't memorized all the distinctions, but I never feel like I'm listening to something I've already heard when I listen to them like I do with some composers whose compositions always seem to be "more of the same".

Bach was king of the keyboard. I've heard several recordings of the Goldbergs, but none surpass Gould. I have four recordings he did of the work – the two studio recordings, one broadcast transcriptions, and one live recording.

The organ works plumb the depths and exalt to the heavens. It's almost as if nothing else should ever be played on the organ, but, of course, then we would miss out on Widor, Franck and others of great power, not to mention the Saint-Saens third symphony.

Probably the orchestral works are the least of the oeuvre. Even so, they are stronger than those of any of his contemporaries. I much prefer them to those of both of his fellow birthday year composers, Handel and Scarlatti. I think they pale a little because Haydn and others came along and took the orchestra places that Bach was not able to go. Of course, his concertos, especially the keyboard, violin and cello ones are works of excellence. I don't have high enough words of praise, so you'll have to provide them.

Tastes change. At different times in my life, I have liked composers to a greater and lesser degree, but I will never grow past Bach.

For more insights on Back see my book, <u>What Does Bach Prove?</u>

3.　　Vivaldi is the brightest of them all. He is the light of the sun. His whole work was radiant, clear through. Bach appreciated him, for I noticed a long time ago that some of his organ works were transcriptions of Vivaldi. This is amazing in a way, as Bach was not much of a world traveler and wouldn't have been exposed to such music in its native venue. So, it was Vivaldi's music which was world traveling.

Vivaldi is the premier composer of concertos. Corelli is often mentioned, but to me he seems to be a far back "also ran" in terms of both the numbers of his compositions and their emotional depth. I like what I have of Corelli, but I don't have much, and I'm not compelled to continually buy more of it.

Vivaldi didn't seem to have done any or many keyboard concertos, at least I don't recall any in the hundreds of his pieces I have recordings of, but the violin and wind instruments are superlative. I particularly like the bassoon concertos. Of course, I've been able to combine my love of Vivaldi with my admiration and respect of Rampal by getting the flute concertos as played by him. The one time I saw Rampal, he played "Il Cardellino". I thought *I* could fly when I heard him. Now, there's a piece that is way too short. But then, maybe Vivaldi knew what he was doing. It's better to leave people wishing you had done more than to leave them wishing you had quit sooner.

In general, I am not enthusiastic over what I have heard of the vocal works of Vivaldi. The Gloria is great, but nothing else that I have heard seems to match it. Of course, I haven't heard everything. My schematic will be enlarged when I hear more.

4.   Stravinsky is a jump in the future, not only from Bach and Vivaldi, but, at times, from where we are right now. He was probably the first modern composer I listened to. He was still alive for the first twenty years of my life, so I could have seen him, but I did not.

Serious, probing, reaching, precise, interior. Those are the words which come to mind when I listen to his music. His is a music of interiors. He was very personal.

I had a lot of Stravinsky's music, but last year I bought a set of 22 discs of his music. This cemented his place in my schematic even more firmly than before. All but two of the disks were conducted by Stravinsky. He played the piano on one of the disks of chamber music. There were pieces I had heard many times before which came to life under his direction. It was as if they became new pieces. We can trust what we hear from the composer because he takes his music personally for by it he makes himself personal to us.

My earliest recollection of his music is "The Rite of Spring". I don't know where I first learned of it. I can vaguely remember Bernstein featuring "Petrushka" on one of the Young Persons' Concerts, but I don't think he did the Rite. By the time I heard it, it was no longer a strange sound world. The dissonances which had caused the riot had become part of the sound stream of the modern consciousness. I was born too late for them to be strange.

I think after that I expected to hear more of the same, especially as "The Firebird" and "Petrushka" seemed to be in working up to "The Rite". I was not prepared for what I heard when I bought my first recording of the "Symphony Of Psalms". There was a great shift. It was not part of the same stream. Then, I found in later years, and even moreso after getting the set conducted by him, that he explored multiple streams and wasn't "more of the same" as many composers were with regard to their schematics. This could be because he was free in the West. By contrast, Dmitri Shostakovich, a contemporary of his who stayed in Russia, seems to have written the same kind of music all his life. Because of the dangerous milieu he operated in, he probably had to play it safe.

There is so much to Stravinsky that never

entered into popular culture. I remember seeing "The Flood" on television in its original broadcast. That may have been the only time I saw Stravinsky on film. I found the "Symphony In Three Movements" to be tremendously suspenseful. The first time I heard it, it seemed as though it belonged in some kind of Hitchcock film accompanying a scene filled with running from danger. That wasn't an intentional programmatic part of the music as far as I know, but the image has lodged itself in my mind and especially endeared that piece to me.

Some of Stravinsky's later works, such as the Mass and other sacred music took a while to work their way into my schematic, but now I listen to those pieces and wonder why I didn't get them the first time I heard them. It just took time to expand my frame of reference or maybe to knock out a few walls in my heart to find room for these pieces.

5.   Then, there are the rest of the Russians. Russian music is soul music, and it is exemplified particularly by Tchaikovsky, Rimsky–Korsakov, Rachmaninov, Glazunov, Shostakovich, and Prokofiev. Also rans include Anton Rubinstein, Myaskovsky, Borodin, Balakierev, Gliere and Glinka.

I could almost exclusively listen to Russian music. This is the deepest expression of the Romantic stream, taking matters much further than Beethoven was able to do. In many ways, it has always seemed the least complicated music of all. Even Shostakovich and Prokofiev seem fairly straightforward as compared to other music from the same era.

Here, in brief, is a paragraph on each of the six exemplary composers listed above.

I probably initially came to know Tchaikovsky through the Disney "Sleeping Beauty" soundtrack. Even now, when I hear a recording of the ballet, I see those scenes. I actually see them more than I do those of Stravinsky's "Rite" sequence from "Fantasia". My next awareness was in the drama of the "1812 Overture". That doesn't seem to be played as much today. When I was shifting my collection from lp to cd, I had a hard time finding a copy of it on cd. It's still an exciting piece, but maybe I heard it too much in my younger days for it to have the same buzz when I play it now. Tchaikovsky is the most brilliant of the Russians, especially in his piano concertos, but for me the height is the 6th symphony, the "Pathetique". It has grown deep roots.

Rimsky–Korsakov, known to most for "Scheherazade", first came into my collection through "The Golden Cockerel" suite. He seems more Russian than Tchaikovsky, and in my thinking is more tied in with show pieces, particularly "The Flight Of The Bumblebee". I like the "Christmas Eve" music. It's not Christmassy as carols are, but I find it reflective in a way that fits the mood of the evening, and for years I have listened to it every Christmas eve.

I have historical recordings of Rachmaninov

playing all four of his piano concertos as well as the "Rhapsody On A Theme Of Paganini". I have never tried my hand at his music, but I can remember one of my music teachers remarking on his octave and a half reach. It would take most of us two hands together to do that. The Vespers give a further depth to his oeuvre which doesn't seem to exist in any of the others Russians. His second symphony, of course, is the cornerstone of my classical experience.

I started collecting Glazunov piecemeal. It began with the "Seasons" ballet music on lp and a violin concerto I heard on the radio. Then, when I started getting cds, I discovered that he had a great presence on Naxos. He was the latest of these first four, and yet, in spirit, he fits with them in a way the next two do not. He may be the last true Romantic composer. His music is definitely in the emotional camp.

Shostakovich was introduced to me on one of the Bernstein programs. They played part of the seventh symphony. A short time after the work was featured on television, I heard it in its entirety on the radio. Because of the way it was spoken of on television, I was expecting something difficult, but I found it very accessible, especially in the part that sounded like a cavalry ride. After that, I think the next piece I heard from him, some years later, was the thirteenth symphony. Being almost a cantata or oratorio in effect, it took a little longer to get used to. I got a recording on Everest Records of the premiere performance. I still have that lp as a historical artifact. You can hear the coughs and crowd commotion on it, but one thing it doesn't have is applause at the end. I always wondered why that was. At present, it is the string quartets which have my attention. I like the tightness of the dialogue.

Like every child of my era, I learned of Prokofiev from "Peter And The Wolf". We heard it at school on record, and I can remember seeing some kind of production of it on television when I was a child. I looked it up online, and what I saw was probably "Art Carney Meets Peter And The Wolf". The date fits my childhood time frame, and the description tallies with what I do recall. Of course, Prokofiev has more to offer than that. I especially like the symphonies and the piano concertos. Some of them are more accessible than others, and they don't go to the heart as much as the earlier Russian composers, but they have a strong place in my schematic.

6. I learned about Bruckner after I learned about Mahler. Mahler came through the sound track of "Death In Venice". It's strange that the film hasn't stayed with me, but the music has. After listening to Mahler, I found Bruckner and started to buy his symphonies. At my first listening to them, when I was in college, I found them to be similar to Mahler's, but as I absorbed all the symphonies of each, the two became disentangled in my mind, and

I gave Bruckner the edge. It is another Haydn/Mozart kind of relationship. I like Mahler, but I love Bruckner. Funny, I seem to esteem higher the one of pair which is less esteemed critically. That's the personal nature of it all.

In the backliner notes of the first album I had of the 9th symphony of Bruckner, which was the work that really won me over, the writer summed up the difference between the two composers in this way. He said that Mahler was searching for God, but Bruckner had found him. I probably let that comment influence me because of my own spiritual background, yet as I kept listening to the two composers, I sensed that he had hit the nail on the head.

Both had a great breadth, and I love the really long symphonies, but Bruckner seems more settled. I was especially influenced by that 9th. The record I had was one I had gotten used from a library sale, but I listened to it more than many of the albums I had which I had acquired in pristine new-out-of-the-shrink-wrap condition. After that, when I got to the cd technology, I replaced it with three more recordings, including one put out by Naxos which has a reconstructed finale. Even though the liner notes always say that the symphony was not completed by Bruckner, it always seemed finished to me in the three movements as we have them. I haven't listened to the extended version as much as I thought I would.

The other symphony of Bruckner's which

looms large on the horizon for me is the 8th. It was one of the first symphonies that I deliberately bought a second version of. It wasn't that I didn't like the one I had, but I saw another on sale in a bargain bin and thought, "I'd sure like to have that." I was glad I got it.

For the most part, I haven't strayed too far beyond the symphonies of Bruckner. It's as though they are a world in their own. I have heard some of the choral work on the radio, but I've never bought it. That may be an area for schematic expansion.

7.   Gottschalk seemed like a funny name when I first heard it. At that time, he was not known at all. A stamp with his likeness on it was decades away. I was introduced to him on the radio. I think this was the first time I was aware that I was hearing someone off the regular repertoire path.

My favorite piece is the "Variations On The Portuguese National Hymn".   It's less than ten minutes long, but it packs a wallop. When I heard the first part for the first time, I even thought to myself, "I could learn to play that", but by the time I got to the end of the piece, that thought was out of my brain.

The piano was Gottschalk's strong point. He overlapped parts of Chopin's and Liszt's life spans in the middle of a century which was the coming of age of the piano concerto. If he had lived longer, I wonder what more we could have had. I think that's one of the marks of a good composer, even one who lived for 80 or 90 years – wondering what we would have gotten if they had done more.

8.   The British aren't coming; they came.

Sometimes in the BBC music magazine, an article writer will bemoan the fact that Britain's home grown composers are not well known outside their borders. That is not the case at all with me. There are seven which I have chosen to group together under this point heading. There are more, such as Walton, Delius, Holst and Britten, who have been bypassed, perhaps unfairly, but which never rose to the levels of those I'm now going to describe. Most of these I was introduced to on the radio, although, like everyone else, I knew Elgar through his graduation march.

I put Arnold Bax at the top of my list. He's not a musical name on the same recognition level as Mozart or Beethoven, but he should be. The first thing of his I heard was the 7th symphony on the radio. Bax seemed a strange name, and having only heard it, I wasn't really sure how it was spelled. Now, I have two complete sets of his symphonies and a lot of his other music. I especially like the tone poems such as "November Woods", cited above as well as his string quartets and the piano sonatas.

Havergal Brian is another blessing from Naxos. They put out his first symphony, the "Gothic", a few years ago. I just saw it advertised in the BBC Music Magazine and looked it up in the store. It lived up to the promise of its name. It was wide and broad and exceptionally emotionally stirring. I hope to get all of his symphonies, but some of them have never been recorded. It's time for the record companies to play catch-up.

Arthur Bliss seemed to have a handle on program music such as the "Checkmate Suite", "The Colours Symphony" and "Adam Zero". When I heard them, they took me somewhere. Then I heard the piano concerto which is the best of what I've acquired of him. His heart seemed to be very light and entertaining. Bliss is a great name for a composer. Everything seems positive with him.

I found out after I started buying the William Alwyn albums on Naxos that he had done soundtrack work for many movies including one of my favorites, "A Night To Remember". I don't think I had ever noticed his name in the credits, and if I had, it wouldn't have registered until after I started getting his symphonic music. Sadly, he wrote only five symphonies. What was he thinking?

I knew Malcolm Arnold, on the other hand, from the films, long before I discovered that he was a composer of symphonies. "The Bridge On The River Kwai" is an example of the synergy of combining a great film with great music. I think lesser music would not have done the film as well. The highlight of his works are his nine symphonies. The few chamber works I have don't seem to be as engaging. It could be that he was not cut out for the intimacy of chamber work, but was perfect for a large canvas with a broad brush. All of the symphonies are worth listening to. I can't say that there is one which rises above the others in my estimation. There is one that has echoes of the Kwai soundtrack, but at the moment I don't remember which one it was.

Edward Elgar is the king of British music. Nothing is so majestic as his marches. In his symphonies, I have found moments reminding me of dramatic sound track music, although I don't think he wrote any soundtracks himself. One of the highlights of the late 90s was the reconstruction of his notes for a third symphony. The BBC Music Magazine released a disc with some of those sketches and a discussion of how it was all put together. I fail to see how any British subject could hear his music and fail to swell with patriotic pride.

Ralph Vaughan Williams left a great orchestral legacy. I enjoyed the sometimes quirky "Job: A Masque For Dancing" before I heard any of the symphonies. It seemed to be something quite unlike anything else when I first heard it. I was impressed by the adaptation of his soundtrack for the film on Scott into a symphony. It remains one of my favorite symphonies, probably because I associate it with my high estimation of the bravery and tragedy of Scott. His story provides more inspiration than that of Amundsen who set foot at the pole first. Vaughn Williams' music captures the character of my perceptions right on. Maybe Scott wasn't so good as this music made him out to be, but I have my doubts as to the proposition that he wasn't.

I have to put in one more. I hadn't intended to include him, but now that I'm at the end of this section, I feel that I must include him. Eric Coates was Britain's equivalent of Leroy Anderson. I learned of him when my high school orchestra played one of his suites. I was forced into that one, but later on, when I began to hear the rest of his music, I was attracted to it, especially the march for "The Dam Busters". I understand that his "Calling All Workers" kept the factories at top production speed during the days of World War II. That song would make me want to do a job I hated.

9.   Charles Ives is America Coming To Grips With Modernism before she was willing to do so. I first heard about him on a Bernstein program, although I'd have come across him sooner or later. At that time in the 1960s, he was virtually unknown, probably even to most adults in Classical Music circles. It's hard and sad to think that one of the most influential modern American composers never heard the bulk of his work performed.

Ives left behind four numbered symphonies as well as the "New England Holidays" symphony. I usually listen to the Holidays one at least once a year on one or more of the Holidays covered – Washington's birthday, Memorial Day, the 4th of July and Thanksgiving. Just a few weeks before writing this comment, I listened to it on the 22nd of

February.

Ives went from being conventional to being himself in the gamut of his symphonies. The two string quartets are fully his. The first string quartet, "From The Salvation Army", the third symphony, "The Camp Meeting", and the fourth violin sonata, "Children's Day At The Camp Meeting", all have a big place in my heart because of his liberal use of hymn tunes. Virgil Thompson, while a much different composer from Ives, also gave us a symphony based on a hymn tune. Today, composers are doing symphonies based on tunes from the output of rock musicians, so it is not out of court to do the same with hymns. By doing what he did, Ives brought the hymns out of the church and into the world at large. He showed that they were not just a side line in life, but a part of the stream of life.

As with Stravinsky, Ives no longer seems as advanced or out of step, although listening to the cd recording "Ives Plays Ives" recorded between 1933 and 1943 you can see how farther out Ives was himself than his interpreters have declared him to be. Hearing the piano works like that, there is nothing to soften the tone. We get the raw Ives. That's usually the case in solo or chamber works as opposed to large scale orchestral works. The individual comes out here, and he is someone I can understand.

I am thankful that Ives has the honor he deserves, but, at the same time, I wonder how many others there are out there or equal merit who are still unknown. Sometimes, the greatest wealth needs to be mined to be reached.

10.   Alan Hovhaness was introduced to me on the radio by "And God Created Great Whales". For years that was all I knew of him. Then, along came the "Mt. Saint Helens Symphony". Actually, it had been written years before I heard it, but it was the recording by the Seattle Symphony orchestra that brought both the symphony and composer out into the open at last. After that, there was no stopping him or me in collecting him.

I will admit that some of his music sounds a lot alike, especially as he wrote so much, but I suppose you could say that about Bach and Haydn, too. What is important is that it sounds like him.

Hovhaness seemed to travel down musical roads not traveled before. He went into areas of his Armenian culture, sometimes even to it's preceding pagan roots. I have listened to those pieces and enjoyed the music without brooding over those roots. I think it is possible to do that without betraying your own philosophy or faith.

I appreciate Crystal Records for espousing his music and keeping it in their catalogue until the rest of the world could catch on. I have many of the recordings on their label as well as the Delos recordings by the Seattle Symphony and the Naxos ones which have added to the available repertoire. Hovhaness will probably never be mainstream like

Beethoven or Bach, but I am glad to be able to get more of his music.

11.   When I first heard of Mexican Classical Music, I dismissed it as being of no importance. Having heard Mariachi music and the hat dance, I figured the most we could get there would be light classics, and there's nothing wrong with those, but I wasn't expecting much more than folk music. Then, I bought a Naxos recording of the music of Silvestre Revueltas and found that I was greatly mistaken.

Revueltas breathed fire and life into music. This was a new emotional take, unlike that from the European or American streams, and it was invigorating and exciting. Then, I discovered that there were other Mexican and Latin American composers of equal stature, and I embraced the music.

Oh, there is lighter music here. Juventino Rosas wrote a piece called "On The Waves" that could very easily be mistaken for a Strauss waltz. Even the hat dance and "La Cucaracha" acquired new life after having been heard through an ear awakened by Revueltas.

On down in South America, Brazil gave us Heitor Villa-Lobos. I had heard the little train in childhood, but once I listened to the entire "Bachiana Brasiliera", I discovered a rich world of music. He also left us with some superb guitar music.

Argentina gave us Alberto Ginastera. I heard his first piano concerto on the radio and was very taken with it, but I hadn't caught the name of the composer. It wasn't until I started exploring this sound world that I discovered his name. A few years ago they featured his harp concerto at the Contemporary Music Festival at Indiana State University. I sat on the front row and swam in it.

There are other Latin Americans that I have a small selection from such as Carlos Chavez and Julian Orbon. This is a part of the schematic that requires more growth. It needs to come to the general attention to a greater degree as well.

12. Krzystof Penderecki is another sound track discovery. They used three of his pieces in "The Exorcist". I didn't particularly like the movie (I don't have a copy of it), but the music, other than one theme, was all from the modern classics. Even though the music was used in film about demon possession, I looked beyond that usage and saw it for what it was. Years later during the 1980s, when I saw a recording of Utrenja at the library and checked it out, I did so because I recognized the name of the composer from the film soundtrack, and because the very title of the piece was intriguing.

At first, I had a hard time with Utrenja, or "The Entombment Of Christ" as it is alternately called. It was probably the most difficult piece of music I had attempted to listen to up to that time.

So much of it just sounded like shouting and noise. It almost seemed as if a bunch of people had just gotten together and sort of wailed as they pleased for 40 minutes. Still, I was determined to master the piece, so I listened to it over and over. A few years ago I found that there was a resurrection part and bought the Naxos recording containing that as well. It's strange, now, but I have a hard time finding the cacophony any more. It is not surprising that the whole of creation would wail at the death and entombment of Christ. We usually pass over the putting of Jesus in the grave, but Penderecki makes that event enormous as it has never before been made enormous. They shout again when He is raised from the dead. This is not "Christ The Lord Is Risen Today", but it is the tremendous power of this event espoused by the music. The sounds of drums and instruments and voices tell us that the significance of this affects all of creation both on earth and even in heaven. It is a cosmic event.

I started to explore his other music, and found much that spoke to me. Penderecki is modern in a completely different way than Stravinsky is. They aren't even traveling on parallel tracks, but going in different directions. Stravinsky is traveling to a goal of self-discovery; Penderecki is traveling to a goal of God involvement. It is that well grounded spiritual base behind his music which I appreciate.

I like the symphonies and choral works

equally well in Penderecki. The chorals, especially, operate in a transport mode. I go somewhere when I hear them. I am waiting for the 6th symphony, though. When number 7 came out, I thought somehow I had missed 6 and started looking for it. I discovered that it had been begun, but not completed at that time. I think I would have labeled what was given to us as his 7th as the 6th and then possibly come back to the material and finished it and given it a new number, but he's kept the number 6 in place, though it has not been completed. I have no idea what it will be like, but I would like to hear it. I've had a hard time tracking down information on it. Some oblique references on the internet seem to indicate that the work has been completed and performed, but not recorded. All I can say is, get with it.

I have read on a liner note or somewhere else that people criticized Penderecki for abandoning atonality for tonality in the middle of his career. I don't see that as a bad thing. A person doesn't have to be committed to one art style forever. In painting, Picasso was known for his "periods". Why shouldn't we allow composers the same freedom, and why does it have to be seen as going backward to come to tonality? Both atonality and tonality are legitimate. I find the fact that Penderecki covers both makes him more interesting and rounded out. He's a real musician and not just a craftsman who can only continually produce the same thing over and over again.

There is one other thing that I have noticed about Penderecki. When I listen to his music, it fills up the space around me. It is not just an adjunct to my day, but it is my day. It has a completeness that I don't always find in other modern composers. Sometimes, I hear them and think about going on to the next thing in my life, but when I hear Penderecki, I am satisfied to be in the presence of his music. He helps me to live in the moment.

13. Geirr Tveitt is another discovery courtesy of Naxos. I don't have as much of his music as I would wish because no one does. Much of it was lost in a fire, but what we do have is great. He is Norwegian, but he is more than simply a copycat of Grieg to be lost in his shadow.

The piano concertos have really captured my attention, particularly number 4 called "Aurora Borealis". I have always been fascinated by the northern lights, even though I've never seen them, so to have a concerto depicting them is not only the next best thing, but a great thing in itself. That's the recording I have listened to more than any other, but his other music has always been fresh and lively.

On the 3rd of February 2013, another aspect of his work came to light when I got a cd of Tveitt's playing of his third concerto. I stumbled across this album online one day and immediately ordered it. It was released on Simax, the same label that had also produced a historic recording of Grieg playing some of his own compositions. I don't have many recordings of composers playing their own works, but they always have power. They give a real sense of connection. That can be seen in the Rachmaninov piano concertos played by Rachmaninov, in Ives' playing of his own works, and the in the conducting of Stravinsky of his own works.

14. Steve Reich is a later discovery. He personally came to the first Contemporary Music Festival I attended. I didn't know he was going to be there in person. I was simply expecting to hear a free string quartet concert which I had noticed as a line item in a local arts magazine.

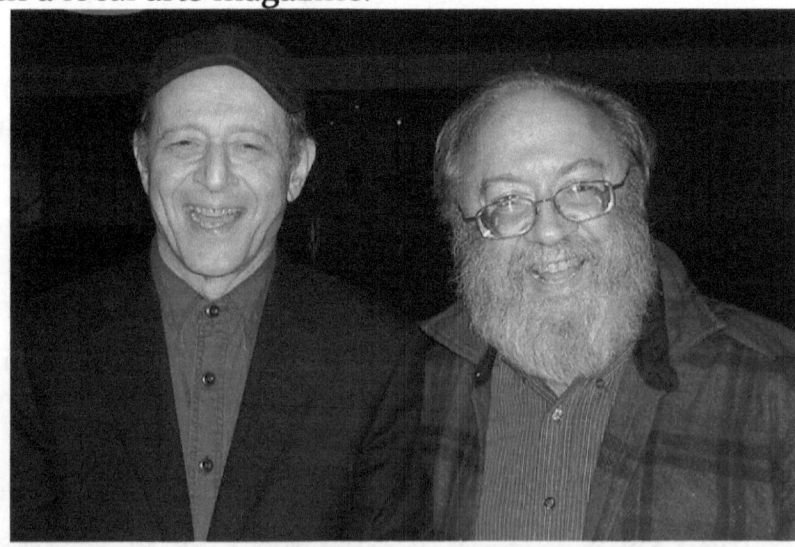

Steve Reich and I on 19 November 2009
I had never heard his music before that night, although I had read about him in the BBC

magazine. Compared to everyone else mentioned in this numbered list, he was way outside any orbit I'd ever flown in. I had heard the music of some of the other minimalists, John Adams and Philip Glass, but when I heard the Triple Quartet played by the Steve Reich Quartet, I knew we weren't in Kansas anymore. I went online the next day and ordered a recording of that piece.

Normally, something like this would take a while to be absorbed into my schematic. Maybe having made myself deliberately expand it in the case of Penderecki's Utrenja, I was able to do so more readily here. I'm not an expert in Reich, but everything I've heard since then, I've liked pretty much from the first listen, although I was prepared for something beyond the pale every time I tried something new.

Reich is not merely repetition, but resonance and resolution. Thoughts are recycled to exhaustion to bring us to their ultimate logical conclusion. Our lives are made up of repetitions which often seem infinitely cyclical, but in his case, the repetition goes somewhere and has a terminus. Life longs for conclusion. Music often takes us to the ultimate, even before we get to heaven. Steve Reich's music has that ability. It is a mixture of threshold and transport.

I couldn't listen to minimalism exclusively. It's not as universal as Bach, which is not intended as a derogatory statement, as I have the highest regard for this music, but it's more like a spice in my musical diet than a staple. The spice can give a punch when needed that the normal does not, but you can't live on it alone. I need more than one type of music to be fully rounded out.

15.   John Philip Sousa had faded way back into the misty recesses of the past. I had heard his music all my life. I attended a concert by the Marine Band when I was in high school, which I'm sure featured a lot of it. I was so used to the marches that I had just about used them up. Then two things elevated my regard for Mr. Sousa.

First, I found out that there was a museum of Sousa artifacts and music at the University of Illinois. It's not in a freestanding building, but in a dedicated floor of one of the music buildings. The great thing was not what was there, but the curator. He had been at the Smithsonian and had come to handle this museum. I've only been there one time, as it's kind of hard parking on campus, but that one fellow made Sousa come to life by the way he spoke of him and personally showed me the exhibits.

It was Naxos, again, which further brought Sousa out into the light. They released three discs of his theater and orchestral music. Among those there were two short works based on hymn tunes. As a result of these three albums, I went back and listened to the other music.

Sousa is not old hat. He was the vitality that defined much of the musical landscape in America. While that wasn't always Classical, it made incursions into the Classical and should keep his music before us. Nothing other than "The Star Spangled Banner" can make us so instantly patriotic, and his patriotism is always uplifting and glorifying.

While he is certainly not the end of my schematic, Sousa makes a good place to round this chapter out with his high and authentic place in our national spirit.

16.   Some Lists

For the most part, in this chapter I will be simply listing some of my estimations of the greatests and my favorites. These lists are not exhaustive. My schematic is alive and bound to be expanded next year, but this is a snapshot of what is there at the present.

Greatest and favorite are not always the same. Greatest is an absolute assessment, although since I'm the one making it, there can't help but be a certain measure of favoriteness involved. To be great, a work must be measured by the entire genre or body of music. In turn, it often becomes the unit of measurement by with other music is gauged. Favorite only means that I happen to like this particular piece better than others. At times, it is hard to keep the concepts apart, but we'll start with the list of what I think are the greatest works in my schematic genres.

THE GREATEST SYMPHONY: Beethoven's 9th

This is the first Beethoven symphony I purchased. I didn't know quite what to expect, but, as it was going to cover two lps, I knew it would be something big and important. No other symphony has the weight and power and universality of this one.

THE GREATEST CONCERTOS: Vivaldi's The Four Seasons

I suppose everyone thinks that, but I'll add my vote to the number.

THE GREATEST CHAMBER WORK: Schubert's Trout Quintet

Even though the string quartet is my favorite kind of chamber work, this piece has always held my attention. It has a life all its own, unlike some chamber works which seem to be only "more of the same". I never get tired of it, and that may be one of the best tests of a "Greatest".

THE GREATEST INSTRUMENTAL WORK: Bach's Preludes and Fugues for the Well Tempered Clavier

I put these above the Goldbergs, not because they are longer, but because they cover so much more ground. I have listened to several recordings by several different pianists, but I don't imagine I could say I have mastered them in that I don't always know what's going to come next. It's amazing how Bach's music can continue to be so fresh.

THE GREATEST CHORAL WORK: Handel's Messiah

As a general rule, I don't "like" Handel anywhere near as much as I love Bach, but this one work of his is the greatest ever. It moves me spiritually and musically. I have ten different recordings of it, and am always open to a new one.

THE GREATEST WORK OF ALL: Handel's Messiah

Were I to be told I was to be set adrift with only one piece for the rest of my lifetime, this would be it.

It's interesting that four of the above six categories contain works not done by my favorite composers. I like Beethoven, Schubert and Handel, but they are nowhere near my like level for Haydn, Vivaldi and Bach. This, in addition to being an example of the triumph of absolute goodness over personal preference, is an example of the veridical. It could be that greatness stands alone rather than as a part of a body of work.

In listing my personal favorites, I would have to admit that it is not as easy to do for some of these categories as it is for the symphonies. I think they are so much more striking in my schematic that they each have a more identifiable presence. The lists for the other genres are more inclusive and not as singular. Many of those will be lists of bodies of work rather than single ones. It's very hard for me to come up with a list for instrumental music, so I have left it alone.

Favorite Symphonies overall in order of preference:

1.   Beethoven #9
2.   Rachmaninov #2
3.   Bruckner #9
4.   Hanson #2
5.   Brian #1
6.   Haydn #44
7.   Saint-Saens #3
8.   Tchaikovsky #6
9.   Shostakovich #7
10. Vaughn Williams #7

The also-rans are too many to catalog.

The string quartet is my favorite form of chamber music. It is impossible to pick out single quartets for listing as I have done with the symphonies. Here are the ten composers whose works appeal to me the most. Haydn is the top; the ones following him are in alphabetic rather than preferential order. It's interesting the large number of those cited which are from the 20th century. This is a medium which matures as it goes. You may note the absence of Mozart's name. I like his quartets, but not as much as I like the others, mostly probably because Haydn so overshadowed him in this field that I want something more different from the others.

1. Haydn
2. Bax
3. Beethoven
4. Boccherini
5. Holmboe
6. Ives
7. Janacek
8. Martinu
9. Villa-Lobos
10. Shostakovich

The piano concerto is my favorite form of concerto. Here are the top ten favorite composers in that form, in alphabetic order:

1.   Bach
2.   Bartok
3.   Beethoven
4.   Busoni
5.   Field
6.   Medtner
7.   Mozart
8.   Rachmaninov
9.   Saint-Saens
10. Tchaikovsky

Vocal music could be simply listing the entire choral output of Bach, but there are others I like as well. I list the specific works I like the most alphabetically, and, as you can see, Bach does predominate.

1. Bach: B minor mass
2. Bach: Christmas Oratorio
3. Bach: St. John's Passion
4. Bach: St. Matthew's Passion
5. Beethoven: Mass in C
6. Handel: The Messiah
7. Haydn: The Creation
8. Penderecki: Utrenja
9. Verdi: Requiem
10. Vivaldi: Gloria

As also rans there are Beethoven's Christ On The Mount Of Olives and his Missa Solemnis, Holst's Hymn Of Jesus, Gounod's St. Cecelia Mass, the Sacred Music of Schubert, Verdi's Four Sacred Pieces, Rachmaninov's Vespers and Steve Reich's You Are (Variations).

ADDING TO THE SEASONS

I listen to music all the time, but I find my enjoyment of a season heightened by the music connected with it. Music adds and brightens. It extends what we are experiencing and makes it more intense. It increases our engagement and involvement. On the popular level, "Jingle Bells" does that for Christmas even though it's not, strictly speaking, a Christmas song; the holidays become more festive when the music is played. On the classical level, these pieces I am going to catalog do the same thing.

Here are some lists which may point to some things you don't know or which you have forgotten with regard to seasonal listening. These are not exhaustive, but are all definite recommendations.

There are several works which cover the seasons as a whole. The most famous is the concerto set by Vivaldi. Others include:

Astor Piazzolla: South American seasons

Alexander Glazunov: The Seasons, a ballet score

Peter Tchaikovsky: The Seasons, a piano cycle

Franz Josef Haydn: The Seasons, an oratorio.

Joachim Raff: Four symphonies, one for each season

Some Pieces Connected With Particular Seasons

Spring:

Alwyn: String Quartet #2 "Spring Waters"
Bax: Morning Song (Maytime In Sussex)
Bax: Spring Fire
Beethoven: Violin Sonata # 5 "Spring"
Bridge: Enter Spring
Copland: Appalachian Spring
Debussy: Printemps
Delius: On Hearing The First Cuckoo In Spring
Goldmark: Im Fruhling
Schumann: Symphony #1 "Spring"

Summer:

Barber: Summer Music
Bax: Summer Music
Bridge: Summer
Honneger: Pastorale D'Ete
Rorem: The End of Summer

Fall:

Alwyn: Autumn Legend
Bax: November Woods
Bax: Red Autumn
Ives: Violin Sonata #2
Resphigi: Autumn

Winter:

Bax: Winter Legends
Bax: Winter Waters
Delius: Winter Night
Holst: A Winter Idyll
Tchaikovsky: Symphony #1 "Winter Dreams

Note: I don't think it's just me. I'd say that composers seem to be more aligned to the season of Spring than any other. It could be that the coming to life of nature every year is a particularly appealing theme which thus gets a lot more coverage. I think it is easier to think of things to write about the coming to life out of slumber, than it is of the deadness of winter. I wish there was more for fall, though, as that's my favorite season.

Other Specific Musical Events And The Pieces Associated With Them

New Year's Day
Bach: Cantatas 153, 190
Herbert: Auditorium March
Recordings of the New Year's Day Concerts in Vienna
Strauss Family

Lincoln's birthday
Abraham Lincoln Portraits cd set by Naxos, which includes the Copland Lincoln Portrait
Diamond: This Sacred Ground
Michael Daugherty: Train Of Tears
Robert Russell Bennett: Abraham Lincoln, A Likeness In Symphonic Form

Washington's birthday
Antheil: McKonkey's Ferry (about crossing the Delaware)
Ives: New England Holidays Symphony

Saint Patrick's Day
Anderson: Irish Suite
Beach: Gaelic Symphony
Harty: An Irish Symphony
Harty: In Ireland
Herbert: Irish Rhapsody
Sullivan: Irish Symphony

Easter and the Passion Week
Bach: Easter Oratorio
Bach: St. John's Passion
Bach: St. Matthew's Passion
Beethoven: Christ On The Mount Of Olives
Boccherini: Stabat Mater
Creston: Symphony # 3 "Three Mysteries"
De Sabata: Gethsemani
Foerster: Symphony #4 "Easter Eve"
Handel: Brooke's Passion
Handel: The Messiah
Haydn: The Seven Last Words (Choral, keyboard, string quartet)
Liszt: Via Crucis
MacMillan: Triduum
Part: Passio
Penderecki: St. Luke's Passion
Penderecki: Utrenja
Pergolesi: Stabat Mater
Stainer: The Crucifixion

<u>American Patriotic Holidays</u> – Memorial Day, Fourth of July, etc.

Note: For these holidays I prefer music really made with America in mind, not simply music written by American citizens. We once attended a 4th of July concert at Carson, California which was touted as a concert of "American Music". It was filled with film music. These were American compositions, and they were very good music, but they was not "AMERICAN" with flags coming out of every letter in the spelling of the word. They didn't embody the idea of Americanness that composers such as Foster, Gershwin, Berlin, Copland and the like do. They know better than that in small town Paris, Illinois. You get the real thing when you go to the 4th of July band concert there.

Bloch: America (the greatest overlooked work in this category)
Gould: American Ballads
Gottschalk: The Union and other piano works
Ives: New England Holidays Symphony
Schuman: New England Triptych
Sousa: every march in his book

<u>Columbus Day</u>
Herbert: Columbus Suite

Thanksgiving Day
Bax: November Woods
Burrill Phillips: Selections From McGuffey's Reader,
second movement "John Alden and Priscilla"
Corigliano: Black November Turkey
Ives: New England Holidays Symphony
MacDowell: A.D. MDCXX (from op, 55)
MacDowell: From Puritan Days (from op. 62)

Christmas

Anonymous 4: The albums "Legends of St. Nicholas", "On Yoolis Night", "A Star In the East"
Bach: Christmas Oratorio and Christmas cantatas
Baroque Christmas edition set by Harmonia Mundi
Britten: St. Nicholas
Fry: Santa Claus Symphony
Gade: Christmas Eve
Handel: The Messiah
Hely-Hutchinson: A Carol Symphony
Honegger: Une Cantate De Noel
Hovhaness: Symphony #49 "Christmas Symphony"
Ireland: The Holy Boy
Leopold Mozart (formerly attributed to Haydn): Toy Symphony
Lutoslawski: Twenty Polish Christmas Carols
MacMillan: Veni
Mathias: Ave Rex
Messiaen: Vingt Regards sur L'Enfant Jesus
Penderecki: Magnificat
Penderecki: Symphony #2 "Christmas"
Praetorius: Lutheran Mass For Christmas Morning
Ramirez: Navidad Nuestra
Rimsky–Korsakov: Christmas Eve music
Rootham: Ode On The Morning Of Christ's Nativity
Rutter: Gloria
Ryba: Czech Christmas Masses
Sheppard: Missa Cantate
Vaughn Williams: Hodie
Vivaldi: Gloria

Not all of these pieces are what seem "Christmassy" to us, but they all have something to say. I was recently listening to the Penderecki "Magnificat". That is a far cry from Bach's and from the familiar carols, yet it lets us know that the story is not only to be found in familiar surroundings of melody and verse, but in truth which lives in every surrounding. Truth does not equal our settings of it. Praise is not merely pleasant, but pressing. It pours out power. I noticed that there was a lot of chaos in the last movement and then out of nowhere almost came the Gloria. Even when our praise is tortured by our condition, it comes to God.

17.   Finale

Why? Why do you have to love it?

Because that's the only way you can get anything out of it. That's the way to experience it and receive its enhancements to your life.

I can't tell you what *you* will get out of it, but I can tell you what *I* have gotten out of it. This is what Classical Music has done in me and to me and for me.

My wife has asked me why I do concert analyses at the end of hearing groups in person. I tell her that the analysis, rather than being an academic exercise, is a way of increasing my involvement in and enjoyment of the music. I'm not so much criticizing as I am incorporating what I have just heard into the schematic of my experience. Some can just listen, say, "I like that," and move on down the road, but I need to do more. Everything fits somewhere inside me when I listen to it. Fitting it in is as necessary as hearing it.

All analysis of any kind is an analysis of ourselves. We are not commenting on what is good or bad in something else, but on what we perceive to be good or bad and why it is of such quality and what that means to us.   It is values which are being tested every time we hear something and think about it.

What does the music do in me? It opens up my mind and spirit.

Music goes with thinking. It keeps me fresh.

It enlivens my outlook. It can express my heartache at times, making it both tangible and manageable. It can liberate from negative feelings and release positive ones into my spirit. When music expresses what I feel, it affirms me and gives validity.

Music can enlarge my capacity for reception in all of life. It is a way of experiencing the untried without being endangered by it.

We often try to understand the universe by looking at it through a pin hole. It's no wonder things don't make sense. We don't have a big enough picture. As I acquire a larger frame of reference, I can act with more confidence and wisdom.

What does music do to me? It allows me to know the good. It makes me look up and beyond where I am. It has even moved me to creation.

I'm a composer of Christian songs. These are simple songs. None of them are what would be considered concert hall literature. I've written over 1900 of them, so I used what Miss Wolff and Mr. Salyer (the orchestra leader who led an informal composition class which I attended in high school) provided as some foundational basics of notation and time and key signatures. I often wished I could compose classical pieces. I did write one once.

It came about after I read a special edition of the BBC Music Magazine dedicated to sacred choral music. I decided I wanted to do something that Bach and Haydn had done, so I followed the traditional text, and, in close to a year, produced a mass. Even though I am not a Roman Catholic, I see this as a musical form which gives credit to God in a mighty way. I have never heard mine performed, but my guess is that it would take about 35 to 45 minutes.

I subsequently tried a few choral settings from the Psalms, but they were nowhere near the level the mass is. I started an oratorio, but it sits in a notebook as a few fragments. Still, I do not regard the unfinished work as in vain. I wrestled with notes and words while I worked on it, and during those moments I lived music.

The arts ought to create a desire to be and to do. The ought to stir and spur. When we create, we can always be ourselves. Our efforts are ours. We make them, and they make us better.

When I hear great music, I go beyond the notes to the heart. That is what always distinguishes greatness. People of great heart are hard to find and harder to be, but we can be them. Music not only liberates from, but, also, to. It is not simply a release, but an empowerment.

What does music do for me? It gives me a break from my current experience. I can hear what they heard at the Thomaskirche and what Esterhazy heard, and I can hear it continuously, via recording, in a way they could not. Music nourishes me.

My heart can feel empty or burdened, but what I hear can change my outlook. It speaks of a different better present beyond my present, of a reality beyond my reality. That's why the slave would sing his Spirituals – to remind himself of what he was going to. He was reminded that there was more than what he knew.

In listening to the twenty-second variation of Rachmaninov's Paganini variations I was struck by the great benefit from the tension and release element of music, especially from music on the emotional side.

That search for release may be what fueled the Sturm und Drang period. It wasn't that they wanted to glorify the storm, but to find some way of grasping it and then possibly managing it. At the very least, the movement was more true to life in that we do experience varied and numerous storms. More often in life, though, we have tension without release.

It is freeing to be rowdy and wild for a time as we have to be so controlled in society. Music allows me to experience strong emotions safely. I like the fact that there is an up and a down or vice versa and that I am not left dangling in that I come to a settled end. My spirit is released in what I hear or play. This doesn't mean that there aren't pieces which leave us in the air, but even those are "safe" because we can walk away from them at will as we can't do from most stress or strife in real life. We can be in charge of what we experience, and thus what we feel in the realm of music.

Music provides a harmless protected venue for dealing with angst or fear. I've read that one of the psychological values of watching some horror movies (I don't think this works for ones that are too graphic or too close to home in terms of a person's own real world experience) is that you can have all the effects of fear without the consequences. It's not that we want to fear, but that we want to be able to experience fear safely in a way that we can walk away from without being harmed. You pass through what you fear.

Art gives credence to our fears that other people don't always do when they tell us, "It's all in your head." Our emotions are validated because they are in the open in the piece of music we are listening to. Someone else knows what they feel because they wrote about it and played it.

To take another art form into consideration, no one can look at Edvard Munch's famous painting, "The Scream", and say that there's nothing wrong with the fellow in the picture. We all know that there is, but we can look his reaction to what we cannot see in the face and not be moved by it. For one moment we are in the room with fear, but not controlled by it. The unseen has no power over us. There is a root of freedom in that moment.

Music does the same for us with a great number of emotions besides fear. I wonder if Beethoven felt better after writing his "Rage Over A Lost Penny"? Even if he didn't, it's great to realize that small losses have seemed great to others as well as to ourselves.

Music has the ability to drain us of our feelings so that we are relieved. We might not be totally unburdened of a particular emotion such as grief, for example, but we can be slowed down in our anguish and brought to a place of more manageable feelings.

Music testifies of peace by its contrasts of tension and resolution. I first noticed this phenomenon in listening to a recording of Rachmaninov's 4th Piano Concerto toward the end of the second movement. The piano rises in intensity and then ascends beyond the conflict to a calm. The notes initially create a sense of unease. Then, everything is changed when a resolution is accomplished.

More recently I found resolution in listing to Clement Janequin's Messe "La Bataille" from the 16th century. This is a part of what we would call early music, but it still speaks to us through the resolution it gives. It allows us to see and think clearly, and when we finish the piece we hopefully take some of that with us.

There are many other pieces in which resolution occurs, especially among the emotional romantics. Take note of the ones that provide resolution for you when you hear them. You may want to go back there when you are needing it later.

Even the music which leaves us in the air has its value. Tonality is good, but even minimalists are seeking for some kind of center. Atonality also serves a purpose, and sometimes I listen to such because it shows what the world is actually like in a state of irresolution. Distressed can express what we feel at times which needs to come to an end and then it ends it by having the piece be over. Even if it is an ultramodern piece which does not resolve, the fact that it does come to an end is comforting.

The ability to end tension in a composition and to complete the circle testifies to the ability to find resolution in life. Music mirrors existence and is true to it, but it does even more.

Music allows me to experience more than I could physically experience in the "real" world. I could travel to Czechoslovakia and never experience what I do from a Dvorak trio. Music not only allows me to go to cultures, but to penetrate the insides of the composers and performers in a way that I could not do through an hour or two of casual conversation in their living presence.

Music enhances and enriches. It allows me to live my life with greater joy and understanding. It adds to me. I would not be what I am today without it. It's not that I am a jumble of notes and time signatures, but that everything I have heard has built me up. I can't imagine the devastation of a world of silence, of a perpetual 4'33". Music helps me to direct myself through the day.

But, what about the collective? What does music do to "us"?

If the musical preferences of others are incomprehensible to us, it is often because the hearts of others are incomprehensible to us. Music can provide a common language and a point of relationship. Sooner or later, we find something defining in music which ties us to others. That always makes for a point of connection. Who doesn't love what connects them with other people, banishing isolation?

I don't know it all. I don't like it all. I don't have all of it in my schematic, but what I know and like and possess, I love.

And you? I can't tell you what the music will do for you. I can only testify to its value. You have to find out for yourself what it can do for you by listening to it. You have to love it... Why? To do you good.

www.ingramcontent.com/pod-product-compliance
Lightning Source LLC
Chambersburg PA
CBHW032024170526
45157CB00002B/848

* 9 7 8 1 3 0 4 1 0 2 7 6 8 *